Top Executive Pay Package

Top Executive Pay Package

Leonard Randolph Burgess

A Joint Publication of
The Graduate School of Business,
Columbia University, and
The Free Press of Glencoe

For information, address: The Free Press of Glencoe,
A Division of The Macmillan Company,
The Crowell-Collier Publishing Company,
60 Fifth Avenue, New York 11
Collier-Macmillan Canada, Ltd., Galt, Ontario

Designed by Andrew Roberts

Library of Congress Catalog Card Number: 63–8414

Dedicated to my wife, Virginia,
whose tireless listening ear and
unending forbearance have been
amazing!

Acknowledgments

The present study arose from a suggestion of Professor Arthur F. Burns that I "do something in the field of executive compensation"—an area sometimes supposed (erroneously) to have been completely explored. His early encouragement and continuing interest in the progress of the study have been most helpful.

Professor Leonard R. Sayles, chairman of my dissertation advisory committee, lent valued assistance in several ways. He showed understanding and patience during the long months of research and computation. In reviewing the repeated drafts of chapters he stimulated me to explore avenues of thought that I had not previously investigated. Moreover, he used incisive editorial surgery without doing material damage to the structure of ideas.

In the early development of several ideas, especially with respect to pension benefits, I am grateful for valuable advice from Mr. G. Warfield Hobbs, III.

Professors Eli Ginzberg, Roger F. Murray, Samuel B. Richmond, Ira O. Scott, and Carl S. Shoup have all made constructive suggestions, which in one way or another are reflected in the work.

The staff of the Public Reference Room of the Securities and Exchange Commission in Washington, of the New York Stock Exchange Library, and of the Butler Library at Columbia have been helpful in making available the necessary public records.

Contents

List of Tables

List of Diagrams

Top Executive Pay Package

Introduction

Contrary to popular impression, little is actually known about the total pay package of the top executive in industry. Even expert thinking about the effects of company policy, as well as the tax and regulatory policies of government, upon the incentives and performance of top executives has been based on fragmentary knowledge of the dynamic changes in trends, composition of the pay package, and pay differentials that have been taking place over the last thirty years. Since 1950, these changes have been especially significant, and even critical. The stock option device in its modern form, for example, has developed since then.[1] A top executive pay package excluding such a major fringe benefit is no longer a realistic measure of what has been, is, or will be happening to the top industrial executive's compensation.

1. A recent study of special value because of its careful analysis of the factors influencing executive mobility, but which nevertheless does not reflect option and other stock plans because the research data did not include years after 1950, is David R. Roberts, *Executive Compensation* (Glencoe: The Free Press of Glencoe, 1959).

The fragmentary nature of our knowledge about the trends in top executive pay is clear from the limited inclusion of pay items in the totals—assuming that totals are shown. The records of the Securities and Exchange Commission, which provide most of the current information on executive compensation, show totals only for "direct aggregate remuneration." The term "total compensation" as used in other studies almost invariably omits both stock option gains and the value of pension benefits,[2] and these are not minor omissions. Deferred bonuses, too, are sometimes omitted altogether from the totals[3] or included by simple addition without allowing any discount for future payment.[4]

Aside from incomplete information on pay measures employed, surveys of top executive pay also suffer from other weaknesses. For example, these surveys usually show data only before taxes, thereby failing to take into account the substantial effect particularly of the federal income tax.[5] Moreover, the heavy emphasis in most surveys on recent year-to-year comparisons[6] has diverted attention from searching out the facts about longer-run tendencies.

In contrast to the way in which top management's total pay package is now treated, is the manner in which union-management negotiations tend to nail down the value of the wages and

2. As to options see, for example, *Executive Compensation,* Studies in Labor Statistics No. 12 (New York: National Industrial Conference Board, 1954), p. 3. SEC records show that in 1956 the unrealized capital gains from stock options of one executive in Aluminum Company of America amounted to more than $1.6 million. On pensions see, for example, the total for the second highest paid executive of Bethlehem Steel in "The Modern Road to Riches: Inheritance and Investment," *U.S. News and World Report* (November 8, 1957), p. 60. This total includes no hint of an income value for a pension which as early as 1952 was estimated at well in excess of $100,000.

3. Nicholas L. A. Martucci and Harland Fox, *Compensation of Top Executives,* Studies in Personnel Policy No. 175 (New York: National Industrial Conference Board, 1959), p. 11.

4. See data for the highest paid officer in General Motors cited in "The Modern Road to Riches: Inheritance and Investment," *loc. cit.,* p. 60.

5. For example, see footnote 3, above.

6. Surveys of this type do provide a useful cross-sectional view of the currently paid part of executive pay at any given time.

2

fringe benefits of the hourly paid worker, even to the third decimal place. One may wonder, if such detailed computations are used by management for the hourly paid worker, why not also for the top executive? If the extras are worth examination at one end of the pay scale, do they not also merit inspection at the other? Not only have executive fringe benefits grown, but critical questions have also been asked about such pay elements as stock options. These remain largely unanswered. It seems likely that in the future the negotiators on both sides of the union-management bargaining table, as well as government policy makers, will be more concerned than heretofore with the top executive's total pay package, including his fringe benefits.

In this study we shall attempt to remedy some of the shortcomings connected with measuring and ascertaining the value of the top executive pay package. New measurement techniques needed to derive a package including not only direct payments but major fringe benefits as well, have been developed. These techniques will be applied to a sample of the largest manufacturing companies in order to trace what has happened to the total pay package over the past three decades. This study will seek to identify the more significant trends both before and after taxes. It will also analyze the more meaningful changes in the composition of the totals. It will investigate too what has been happening to pay differentials in the upper echelons of top management. Finally, we shall be concerned with the broader implications of the results.

In order to develop the more significant trends in connection with the top executive pay package, as well as to probe the wider implications of the trends, we had first to select a sample to which the new techniques of measurement might be applied. Choosing the sample involved problems as to which companies, which executives, and which years should be sampled.

Companies to be sampled were chosen on the basis of size, homogeneity, and stock exchange listing. Size was taken as the chief criterion, both because of the influence of the larger companies on the economy in general, and because of their more

3

specific role in setting the patterns for wage and salary trends. Some idea of the importance of the largest companies to the economy as a whole can be gleaned from the fact that the total assets of these companies accounted for about one-quarter of the corresponding total for all manufacturing corporations.[7]

Aside from the general economic importance of the largest companies, their influence on the development of new pay practices is important. Despite the large extent of individual bargaining between companies and executives, personnel practices affect the pay of executives as well as that of other employees of a firm. There has been an increasing tendency for companies to install pay plans that cover all employees, and even the more exclusively executive pay items such as stock options tend to crawl farther down the pay ladder than was once the case.

Homogeneity, the second criterion of company selection, was used because a cross section of all corporations would show great variation in pay practices. For instance, railroads and utilities are subject to a greater degree of government control and have other characteristics that distinguish them from manufacturing companies. Thus pay practices in such concerns differ materially from those in manufacturing. The same can be said for retail and wholesale trade concerns, whereas within manufacturing there is a high degree of homogeneity.

Listing, the final criterion, was necessary because only those firms listed on organized stock exchanges are required to file information on their executives' pay with the SEC. After a consideration of all three criteria—size, homogeneity, and listing—the 25 largest manufacturing corporations listed on the New York Stock Exchange were selected as the sample of companies for the present study.

In selecting the companies we decided to use the 25 which were the largest in each year, rather than work with the same

7. The total for all manufacturing corporations was close to $166 billion in 1952, according to National Industrial Conference Board, *The Economic Almanac 1953–54* (New York: Thomas Y. Crowell, 1953), p. 342. That for the largest companies was roughly $40 billion.

4

companies for the whole 1929–1958 period. The identical company approach would have year-to-year consistency; yet it would not reflect adequately the significant changes in the composition of the top 25 firms which took place between 1929 and 1958. Companies such as Armour, Swift, and International Paper, prominent in early years, have not been in the top 25 in recent years. On the other hand, International Business Machines,[8] not even in the top 100 in 1929, climbed into the top 25 in 1957 and stayed there in 1958.

A detailed description of the method of putting the sample together is given in Appendix I. An alphabetical listing of the firms, showing the years for which they are included in the sample is presented in Appendix II.

The key to the selection of executives for our study was the availability of source material on their pay. Information on the pay of top executives can be obtained from the SEC, the Federal Trade Commission, the Treasury Department, and, of course, from surveys conducted from time to time by private industry and educational institutions. Aside from one or two surveys which are either based on confidential information or cover only a limited number of years or companies, most of the nongovernmental studies are secondary sources of information.[9] Since the original source for all years except 1929 is the SEC, the choice of executives for whom pay information was to be gathered was largely determined by SEC regulations. Under these regulations, corporations are required to report facts about compensation with respect to

8. A. D. H. Kaplan's lists of the 100 largest industrials, based on asset size, were used extensively. See his *Big Enterprise in a Competitive System* (Washington: The Brookings Institution, 1954), pp. 145–155. Also used were lists of 100 largest manufacturing companies prepared from time to time by the First National City Bank and by the National Industrial Conference Board, Inc.

9. For example see Arch Patton, "Annual Report on Executive Compensation," *Harvard Business Review*, Vol. XXV, No. 5 (1957), pp. 125–136. See also *Executive Compensation* and *Compensation of Top Executives*, Studies in Labor Statistics Nos. 12 and 17 (New York: National Industrial Conference Board, 1954 and 1956).

each director, and each of the three highest paid officers, of the issuer whose direct aggregate remuneration exceeded $30,000, naming each such person.[10]

The terms "director" and "officer" as used above are broadly defined. A "director" means

any director of a corporation or any person performing similar functions with respect to any organization whether incorporated or unincorporated.[11]

An "officer" means

a president, vice president, secretary, treasurer or principal financial officer, comptroller or principal accounting officer, and any other person performing similar functions with respect to any organization whether incorporated or unincorporated.[12]

"Direct aggregate remuneration" typically includes salaries, directors' fees, and currently paid bonuses. Other parts of the regulations, however, do require the reporting of additional information on such pay items as pensions, options, deferred bonuses, and deferred fixed cash payments under contract. The $30,000 limit on direct aggregate remuneration is a step-up from a former limit of $25,000 and a still earlier limit of $20,000. This point is not material, since all of the highest paid executives among the 25 largest manufacturers have consistently received direct aggregate remuneration well in excess of these limits.

In recent years, some of the largest companies have reported compensation data to SEC for other executives in addition to the top three. For many firms, though, especially in the earlier years, compensation was reported only for the three highest paid. For this reason, the inclusion of executives in our study has been limited to the three highest paid officers. In general, directors are included only where the amounts paid to them as officers would rank them among the three highest paid.

For the year 1929 only, selection of the three top men was

10. U.S. SEC, *General Rules and Regulations under the Securities Exchange Act of 1934, As in Effect January 10, 1958,* Item 7 (*a*)(1).

11. *Ibid.,* Rule 405.

12. *Ibid.*

6

based on FTC data. These data are the only ones available on top executive compensation in 1929 that are also comparable to the later SEC data.

In selecting the sample years, the data published by the United States Treasury on the compensation of corporate officers[13] provided a useful guide. The Treasury's figures are for the compensation of all officers (not merely the three highest paid) and presumably represent the expense chargeable currently by the companies against income on their corporation income tax returns. The data can thus be considered as representing mostly current outlays.

Using peak years as a rough guide and after examining other factors such as the availability of records, the following years were selected: 1929—a year of prosperity, covered by reports to the FTC; 1937—a prewar year under SEC reporting; 1942—a prosperous year under wartime controls; 1948—a year of post-World War II prosperity; 1952—a year of Korean War prosperity and wage and salary stabilization; and 1955–58—recent years.

Having resolved the problems of sample selection—which companies, which executives, and which years—we then had to consider the contents of the executive's pay package that we were going to measure. The items of principal interest in the top executive pay package differ from those for hourly paid workers. In the latter case, it is appropriate to consider fringe benefits affecting a large number of employees, and the data are averages. Pay package data at the upper end of the compensation scale, however, are more in the nature of individual calculations since there are so few people in these brackets. The sorts of pay items also differ. Those items which will be included in the top executive pay package do not necessarily apply for any one firm, since they vary from company to company. These items are: salaries; bonuses (current and deferred, also stock and cash); dividends on

13. U.S. Treasury Department, *Statistics of Income, Corporation Income Tax Returns* (Washington: U.S. Government Printing Office, 1929–1954), Table 2, Receipts and Deductions for latest years shown.

undelivered stock; pensions; deferred cash under contract; thrift and savings plan benefits; and stock option and purchase gains. We shall exclude, as do most surveys of executive compensation, executive expense accounts; life insurance premiums; stock and debenture subscription gains; and gains from management trusts.

Each of the pay items included in the package will be analyzed and evaluated in our study, and even those excluded from our analysis will be discussed. The effects of taxes on the executive pay package, and management's attempts to offset them, will be investigated. Finally, we shall look at the significance of the trends our study reveals and consider what their future influence may be on such matters as executive performance, government regulatory and tax policy, and the distribution of income among different occupations in our society.

I

Salaries

Salaries in the context of our study have a twofold importance. First, they still constitute the largest and most significant part of the top executive pay package,[1] and for this reason we shall be concerned with salary trends in the aggregate, as are many other surveys of executive compensation. On a second count, however, salaries are even more important—in the determination of the income values of pensions, deferred cash payments, and deferred bonuses, through the use of career salary curves, which will be estimated for each executive. Their estimation is necessary because income values of pensions and deferred cash payments involve the determination of what proportion of his pay an executive would otherwise have to set aside in order to buy his post-retirement benefits. The proportion is determined largely by the

1. Salaries also have a symbolic value in the sense that they are used as one means by which different levels of authority and responsibility are given recognition within the corporate structure. We are not here concerned with this particular aspect.

9

shape of his salary curve. The salary curve data also make it possible to estimate pension benefits for the large number of executives for whom no pension estimates were reported to SEC. After-tax income values, if they are to be realistic, must reflect the tax rates and deduction rates which are imposed on all of an executive's income received in his capacity as a corporate executive. On deferred bonuses, for example, an executive might receive in the same year an annual installment from each of five different bonus awards in addition to his salary.

Trends in Salaries

Salary trends for the three highest paid executives in all of the 25 largest manufacturing companies taken together are shown in Diagram 1, both before and after taxes, for each of the years in the sample—1929, 1937, 1942, 1948, 1952, and 1955–1958. The data are plotted on a ratio scale which is useful in comparing percentage rates of growth. On this type of scale, if two lines move upward a steeper slope indicates a greater percentage increase, while a sharper downward slant in one line rather than the other would mean a larger percentage drop. Certain conclusions may be drawn from the diagram: before taxes, salaries of the three highest paid officers taken together have made a slow, almost uninterrupted climb over the period 1929 to 1958, from less than $5.5 million to well over $11 million. After taxes,[2] salaries, which held steady through 1937, were sharply reduced in wartime 1942 to less than $3 million. Despite the general upward movement since then, in 1958 they were, at $5.5 million, not much higher than the $4.7 million level of 1929.[3] The widened gap between the before- and after-taxes lines, while nar-

2. Taxes refer to the federal individual income tax.

3. If the movement of the consumer price index over the 1929–58 period were also taken into account, the average executive's salary after taxes in terms of real income would be less than in 1929. Other pay package items would also be affected.

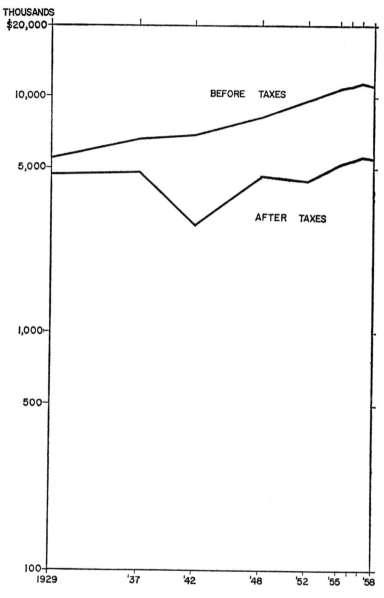

THOUSANDS

$20,000

10,000

BEFORE   TAXES

5,000

AFTER   TAXES

1,000

500

100

1929   '37   '42   '48   '52   '55   '58

Diagram 1—Salaries, Top Three Together

11

rower now than in 1942, demonstrates an increasingly heavy impact of taxes on the salary part of the pay package.

As an example of the calculations involved, we may use the case of an executive in the Anaconda Company. The officer received in 1958 salaries and fees amounting to $185,000. For the purposes of our study, since no other income was received by him from the corporation, the amount given was considered to be his adjusted gross income. Deductions of 18.3 per cent were applied. Multiplying by the complement or 81.7 per cent, the taxable income was a little over $151,000. The tax rate at this level worked out to 60.7 per cent,[4] giving a tax of about $92,000. This left a salary total after taxes of roughly $93,000.[5]

Having looked at the growth aspects of salaries, let us now observe their relative importance as a part of the total pay package. This is shown in Table 1.

Table 1—Salaries as Per Cent of Total Pay Package

Year	Before Taxes	After Taxes
1929	43.5	45.0
1937	74.1	76.7
1942	71.1	71.7
1948	60.9	63.6
1952	54.5	50.8
1955	37.5	32.5
1956	38.2	32.8
1957	49.7	46.4
1958	55.5	52.0

From Table 1 we can conclude that salaries, both before and after taxes, have always accounted for a large share of the total pay package. The 1958 percentages, while below the highs of 1937, were not only higher than those of 1929, but also far above the lows of 1955 and 1956. The low percentages of 1955 and

4. In general, deductions rates were based on U.S. Treasury Department, *Statistics of Income, Individual Income Tax Returns* (Washington: U.S. Government Printing Office, various years). Tax rates used assume a married couple with two dependents.

5. For many companies tax calculations were somewhat more complicated due mainly to overlapping of income or to additional payments in the form of bonuses.

1956 are explained by the heavy exercise of stock options during those years. In the period 1929–1948 the percentages after taxes were somewhat higher than those before taxes, because items other than salary, especially bonuses, were taxed more heavily. From 1952 on, just the reverse was true. The after-tax percentages ran behind. During these years, low capital gains rates applying to stock option gains left options with a larger share, salaries with a smaller share, of the after-tax total.

The Top Executive's Career Salary Curve

The problem of approximating the shape of the top executive's career salary curve involves the estimation of unknown portions of the curve. For most of the 25 largest companies, the present study includes salary data for only a few selected years after the officer has already reached the upper rungs of the organizational ladder. We know little of what happened to salaries before this time, or of what happened or will happen after the known salary years. However, by utilizing information about when executives in our study started to work and the approximate level of starting pay, procedures can be developed by which career salary curves can be estimated for each top executive.

For each of the three highest paid executives in the 39 firms included in one year or another among the 25 largest, certain elements of personal information were gathered as part of our research. For smaller firms, such information—consisting of facts like year of birth, year when the executive joined the company, and year of retirement and/or death—is not generally available. But for the larger companies, it is available, although it has to be gathered from a number of different sources.[6]

As a result of the collection of these personal data, it has been possible to calculate for top executives the age at which each offi-

6. *Who's Who in America, New York Times Index* and microfilms, and other sources such as company annual reports.

cer started work with one of the nation's 25 largest manufacturing companies. This is shown in Table 2.

Table 2—Age First Started Work with One of 25 Largest Companies[a]

Age	Executives
Up through 15	9
16 to 20	25
21 to 25	79[b]
26 to 30	41
31 to 35	28
36 to 40	32
41 to 44	11
45 to 49	18
50 to 59	11
60 and over	0
Total	254

[a] Includes predecessor firms in a few cases.
[b] Distribution within this group for successive ages: 19, 17, 15, 17, and 11.

From Table 2 we can reasonably conclude that a plurality of executives started to work for one of the largest companies between the ages of twenty-one and twenty-five (the modal age group), and that the age distribution within this group was fairly even. Only a few executives went to work at age twenty or younger. If the analysis were confined to those executives who had their start in more recent years, the number would be even smaller. A substantial number of executives joined one of the largest companies while in their thirties, forties, and fifties, presumably coming from other firms and other occupations after a much earlier start at earning a living.[7]

If we did not have the actual tabulation, it would still seem reasonable to assume that the typical executive might be graduated from high school at age eighteen and from college at age twenty-two. This age falls within the modal age group of twenty-one to twenty-five noted above. Also indicated above, a few executives started to build their salary curves by joining their compa-

7. It should also be noted that no executive in the study was recorded as starting with one of the largest companies at age sixty or over. This would appear to be more evidence of the serious social problem inherent in management hiring policies, which too often fail to recognize ability in older men.

1 4

nies at an earlier age. Those officers who did not join until later can be presumed to have started their earning careers earlier—say, at age twenty-two—so that they joined the largest companies at salary levels far above normal starting salaries. On this basis, we have assumed that each executive's point of origin for salary purposes is at age twenty-two, or the year he joined one of the largest companies, whichever occurred first.

The collection of personal data on top executives also provides useful assistance in arriving at a level of starting pay at the point of origin. This can be seen in Table 3, which shows for 301 executives when each executive joined his company and the prevailing levels of wages.

Table 3—When Executive Joined the Company and Average Earnings in Manufacturing

Year Joined Company	EXECUTIVES JOINING COMPANIES			AVERAGE EARNINGS PER EMPLOYEE IN MANUFACTURING[b]	
	Before Adjustment	Partial Adjustment[a]	After Adjustment	Low	High
1880–85	4	—	4	$ 443	$ 479
1886–90	10	—	10	473	498
1891–95	21	—	21	438	506
1896–00	22	—	22	460	493
1901–05	31	—	31	517	560
1906–10	20	—	20	538	633
1911–15	34	+3	37	609	657
1916–20	54	+2	56	738	1,539
1921–25	36	+3	39	1,303	1,541
1926–30	25	+4	29	1,484	1,543
1931–35	19	+1	20	1,086	1,369
1936–40	11	+1	12	1,287	1,432
1941–45	4	−4	—	Not Relevant	
1946–50	5	−5	—		
1951–55	5	−5	—		
Totals	301	—	301	—	—

[a] Partial adjustment reflects reclassification of each late-starting executive who joined one of the largest companies in 1940 or later, but who reached age twenty-two in an earlier year. Reclassification was on the basis of the year when the officer reached age twenty-two.
[b] Data are a combination of four series linked together at 1929, 1926, and 1890. The series represented are: the U.S. Dpartment of Commerce's average annual earnings per full-time employee in manufacturing; the National Industrial Conference Board's average weekly earnings in 24 manufacturing industries; Paul H. Douglas's average annual earnings of wage earners in manufacturing; and another series going back to 1860 for average wages per day in nonagricultural establishments.

From Table 3 it can be deduced that there was a heavy concentration of executives joining the largest companies in the periods from 1911 to 1930. During the single period 1916–1920 one out of every six executives included in the survey joined one of the 25 largest manufacturing firms. By contrast, only a small number of top officers joined these companies after 1935. In fact, when even a partial adjustment is made to allow for late starting executives, the intervals after 1940 disappear altogether.

Another aspect of the table merits equal attention. This is the course of average earnings in manufacturing. For each period only the highest year and the lowest year are shown in the table. For the entire period 1880 to 1940, yearly earnings were never lower than $438 nor more than $1,543. And during the period of greatest concentration of hiring, 1916–1920, the range was somewhat narrower, $738 to $1,539. This range roughly brackets the $1,000 earnings level. On the assumption that for the period 1880 to 1940 future executives were hired at close to the average earnings figure in manufacturing, those hired before 1916 would be hired at somewhat less than $1,000 a year, and those after 1920 at a little more than $1,000 annually. Thus for purposes of building salary curves in the present study a rough figure of $1,000 a year has been assumed as the starting pay for each executive at his point of origin.

The assumption of a point of origin for each executive makes it possible to compare salary curves. This is done in Diagram 2, which shows the curves for the three highest paid executives in one of the 25 largest manufacturing concerns. There are more than three lines since the officers included represent those at the top of the ladder in more than one of the sample years.

The vertical scale is semilogarithmic, which has particular advantages when we wish to look at the rate of growth. That is, if a line is steeper, it means that the percentage rate of growth is greater. Conversely, a tendency for the line to rise more slowly indicates a lesser percentage of increase. The horizontal scale, instead of indicating calendar or fiscal years, shows the years since the zero point or point of origin. To illustrate the working of the scales, let us use the officer shown by the highest reaching line in the diagram. This individual joined the company at an

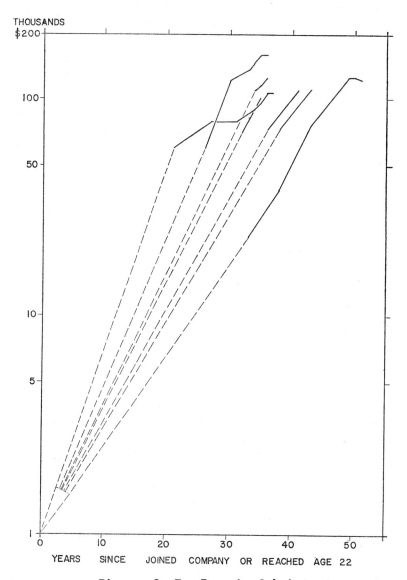

THOUSANDS

**Diagram 2—Top Executive Salaries
for One of 25 Largest Manufacturers**

YEARS   SINCE   JOINED   COMPANY   OR   REACHED   AGE   22

17

arbitrary $1,000 at year zero. From this point of origin his curve extends diagonally upward to reach the first recorded salary figure of $60,000 after 26 years with the company. After 30 years from his point of origin, he had reached $120,000. He kept on climbing to reach a level of $160,000 after 35 years with the firm.

From the paths traced by the solid lines in the diagram, which represent actual salary data, it is clear that salaries tend to rise. They do not remain at the same level until retirement, as is typically assumed in the pension estimates reported in proxy statements. The dashed lines in the diagram can be taken as a rough measure of the average percentage rates of growth for the period before the recorded salary curves, even though the actual rate during these unknown years must have been sometimes greater, sometimes smaller, than these approximate tracings. But the evidence is clear that in each case the path of the actual salary tends to bend to the right, compared to the average percentage performance of the past. This of course indicates a slowing down in the rate of growth.

Having examined the actual salary curves for the meager evidence they provide as to behavior during years of recorded salary, we are now in a position to carry the analysis further and to inquire more closely into two questions: (1) What is the probable shape of the lower tail of the salary curve, extending from the year of origin to the time when actual data are first recorded? (2) What is the most likely form of the upper tail of the curve which extends from the latest recorded actual figure to the time of retirement?

The problem of the lower tail is one of resolving the question of what happens to the executive's salary between the time he is paid an assumed $1,000 at his year of origin and the time, say, 26 years later, when he is paid $60,000. What then is the real shape of the lower tail?

It will be helpful in considering this question first to look at some of the theoretical alternatives and then to see what some of the indications are from company personnel practices. While in theory there could be almost any number of assumptions as to the mathematical curve approximated by the lower tail, it will be sufficient here to look at two of the more obvious possibilities. These are shown in Diagram 3, which uses the same types of scales as Diagram 2.

Diagram 3 shows the picture of a hypothetical executive who is paid $121,000 after 40 years with his company. It shows the lower tail as it would appear, first assuming an arithmetic rate of increase of a flat $3,000 each year, and second assuming a compound interest rate of increase of 12.7 per cent. Which of these two curves is closer to reality? The difference at any particular time can be substantial. For example, when the hypothetical executive has been with his company for 20 years he would be earning $11,000 if his salary followed the compound interest line, against $60,000 if it followed the arithmetic rate of increase.

In a test of the two curves, partially known salary data and actual pension plan provisions for a number of executives were used to calculate estimated pension benefits. An arithmetic rate of growth similar to the bow-shaped curve in the diagram was used for the lower tail of the salary curve while the typical proxy statement assumption of continued salary at the same level to retirement was used for the upper tail.[8] These calculations resulted in estimates generally far in excess of the proxy statement data.

In view of the foregoing outcome of the pension calculations, they were next recalculated using the other assumption as to the lower tail of the salary curve—that is, a compound interest rate of increase of a fixed percentage each year, like the straight line in the diagram. The new assumption gave calculated benefits which were much closer to the benefits reported in proxy statements.

8. This assumption, earlier shunned as unrealistic, nevertheless had to be used here in order to place the calculated benefits on a basis comparable to the proxy statement data.

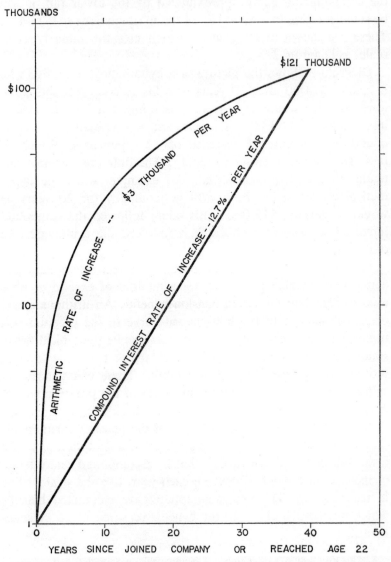

THOUSANDS

$100-

$121 THOUSAND

\$3 THOUSAND -- PER YEAR

ARITHMETIC RATE OF INCREASE

COMPOUND INTEREST RATE OF INCREASE -- 12.7% PER YEAR

10-

1

0   10   20   30   40   50

YEARS SINCE JOINED COMPANY   OR   REACHED AGE 22

Diagram 3—Two Theoretical Assumptions as to the Lower Tail

20

Further indication of the probable nature of the lower tail of the curve is provided in personnel practices with regard to how salary increases are given in the largest companies. For example, it is typical that a man at a lower salary level is given a smaller amount of increase, say $25 a month, while $500 a month would be more typical at a higher level. Thus considering the course of a future executive's career salary curve, rising increments along with rising salaries appear to point away from the constant dollar amounts of increase as implied in the bow-shaped curve in the diagram and toward the compound interest percentage rate of increase shown by the straight line.

Turning now to examine the upper tail of the executive's career salary curve, let us look back to Diagram 2. It will be recalled that the period for which actual salaries were available indicated a slowing down in the rate of growth compared to the average past percentage rate of advance. Thus if the curves are projected farther into the future to the date of the officer's retirement, the implication of the known facts would be either a projection at the latest known percentage rate, or perhaps one at a rate reflecting a continuation of the slowdown in the rate of increase. One way of reflecting this would be to use an arithmetic rate for the forward projection.

On considering the likely future performance of a curve, one ought to look not merely at the possible mechanical extrapolation but also at causal factors. Are there, for example, any bits of evidence that might argue for a roofing-off of salaries at the upper levels? There are in fact some indications that this may be the case. For an executive who is climbing up the ladder, the pay differentials between organizational ranks constitute an important spur to ambition. But it can be argued that when an executive reaches the top three he is on the upper rungs of the ladder. He has arrived, and further incentives are not as important as they were earlier. New factors also come into play, such as responsibility to the public, and the fact that enormous salary hikes get wide public scrutiny. These facts suggest once more a slowdown in the rate of growth at the upper end of the top officer's salary curve.

In evaluating the shape of the upper tail of the salary curve, the form of the projection may not be too critical if the number of years until the year the executive is expected to retire is small. It is one matter if the projection involves a five-year period. It is quite another if, as is often the case, the projection may run 15 to 25 years into the future. Take the instance of an executive in a metal manufacturing concern who had 21 years to go until retirement. Forward projection of the salary curve on the basis of the latest known percentage rate of advance would result in a salary at the time of retirement of approximately $10 million, and use of the average percentage rate rather than the latest one would produce about the same result. By contrast, if the same executive's average past rate of advance, stated as the absolute increase in dollars per year were used, the officer's pay would reach only the more reasonable figure of $210,000.

The evidence seems to point to a curve which shows a rather rapid rise in the years before the executive reaches the top three, a slower rate of advance when he enters this elite group, and probably a further slowing down in the rise during the years beyond those of known salary data. The evidence, however, is subject to widely differing interpretations because of the lack of publicly accessible information for the full length of the career pay curve. For example, it may actually be that the true shape of the entire career salary curve is best portrayed by a logistic or Gompertz curve. Such a curve can be described as starting at a low rate of advance, gradually speeding up to a rapid rate of climb, and then slowing to a less rapid rate of increase in the years closer to retirement.

In theory it would also be desirable to modify such a theoretical curve to reflect cyclical ups and downs, and of course such a modification would result in a more accurate approximation to reality. It is fair to observe, however, that even after 1929, reductions in pay among the highest paid officers in the largest companies usually took the form of cuts in bonuses rather than

22

reductions in salary.[9] The additional complexity of introducing cyclical changes into the curve would not appear to be warranted by the degree of accuracy of the data in the present study. It is also doubtful if the effect would be material to the final results.

Whatever may be said of the theoretical shape of the entire career salary curve of the executive, it still must be affirmed that the data available for the more than 200 executives in the present study actually cover only a small segment of the salary curve. There does not appear to be much justification for using elaborate mathematical curve-fitting techniques in view of this fact. Practical considerations dictate a simpler approach, the use of the compound interest rate of increase for the lower tail of the curve, the use of the actual data for the years of known salary, and the use of the arithmetic rate of increase for the upper tail.[10]

Putting this method into practice, here is an example of calculating the lower tail. For one executive, pictured in Diagram 2 as the highest reaching curve, the known salary was $60 thousand after 26 years with the company. The lower tail was constructed by taking only two more points from the dashed line extending back to the point of origin—$4.8 thousand after ten years, and $23.3 thousand after 20 years. The in-between years were obtained by arithmetic interpolation. For example, salary in the first ten years rose from $1 thousand to $4.8 thousand, an increase of $3.8 thousand. This divided by ten years gave an annual in-

9. John C. Baker, *Executive Salaries and Bonus Plans* (New York and London: McGraw-Hill, 1938), p. 242.

10. In certain cases estimation of the upper tail resulted in a projected figure higher than the third highest paid for a year when this executive did not fall into the top three and where additional income such as bonuses would not explain the discrepancy. In such cases the estimate for the upper tail was lowered. Otherwise this officer would have appeared among the top three for the year in question.

In a limited number of cases a lower figure was arbitrarily substituted for the high which would be reached at retirement by using the average arithmetic past rate of increase. The new figure was estimated by considering such bench marks as the highest figure ever reached by the company, or the highest figure reached in a later period if that seemed more reasonable. In about three cases an arbitrary ceiling of $250,000 or $300,000 was used.

crement of $.38 thousand. This increment was then used to fill in the gap years, with each figure rounded. Thus the first ten years after the year of origin were in thousands of dollars: 1.4, 1.8, 2.1, 2.5, 2.9, 3.3, 3.7, 4.0, 4.4, and 4.8.

In the example above, it is clear that the pure mathematical curve was violated in the sense that instead of reading off all the points, we used only every tenth year and then used arithmetic interpolation in between. This, however, serves as a good approximation for all practical purposes. It also saves much work and possible error in the reading off of endless numbers of points.

We shall not give any example for the years of actual salaries as the method of interpolation is the same. The difference lies in the use of actual salaries as bench marks instead of data from a semilogarithmic plot.

To demonstrate projection of the upper tail we can use the same executive as we did for the lower tail. His latest known salary figure was $160 thousand. This was $159 thousand in excess of the assumed starting salary of $1 thousand. The $159 thousand divided by 36 years elapsed gave an average annual career rate of advance (arithmetical) of $4.42 thousand. The upper tail was extended by adding increments, as follows (in thousands of dollars): 160.0, 164.4, 168.8, 173.3, 177.7, 182.1, 186.5, 190.9.

Now that we have established a method for the construction of career salary curves, we can employ this essential tool in discovering the income value of pensions, deferred cash payments under contract, and deferred bonuses, all important items in the executive's pay package. They will be discussed in the next two chapters.

II

Bonuses

Since the three highest paid executives in each of the largest companies are in a position on the organizational ladder where their decisions can have a direct, visible effect on the profitability and growth of the company, they are often paid bonuses in addition to salary. The theory is that these will serve as an incentive to spur management to greater effort which will be reflected in improved performance of the firm. A question naturally arises as to whether bonuses are often merely a substitute for salary. Later, in discussing the size of the bonus, we shall explore this matter. First, however, we shall examine two other aspects of bonuses: the determination of income values of deferred bonuses, and an analysis of the trends in bonuses for the 25-company sample over the 1929–1958 period.

Income Values of Deferred Bonuses

Currently paid bonuses in cash or stock, like salaries, involve relatively simple problems of income determination.[1] This is not true of deferred bonuses. The latter, whether paid over a period of years following the award (short-term deferment), or distributed over the years after retirement (postretirement deferment), entail a host of complexities. In some studies of executive compensation these bonuses have been added to salaries and treated as current income, which they are not. In others, they have been omitted altogether, which is unrealistic. For purposes of analysis in our study, the problems connected with these bonuses will be grouped into those relating to the value *now* of income payable in the *future,* and those having to do with the overlapping of income.

We shall include deferred bonuses in the top executive pay package at income values which reflect the fact that income which will be paid in the future is at present worth less than the same amount paid currently. Or putting it in reverse, we can speak of the present value of the future income. To determine the present value, it is necessary to assume a rate of interest and also to know something about the nature of the income—whether it is to be paid in a single lump sum or in installments. When we know the present value, we shall be able to show how it can be applied to determining the income values of deferred bonuses.

In choosing an interest rate there are two possible approaches. One is to assume that funds are invested in tax-free securities.

---

1. The chief problem in connection with the currently paid bonus is the determination of income after taxes. For the typical company, salary and bonus are added together to arrive at adjusted gross income. This is multiplied by a factor to allow for deductions, and the result is multiplied by an appropriate tax rate to determine the amount of the federal individual income tax. The amount of the tax is then prorated between salary and bonus, and after-tax figures are obtained by subtraction. No distinction need be made between cash and stock when paid currently, since both are equally taxable and no appreciation takes place in the value of the stock.

2 6

The other is to assume that funds are invested in a corporate trust fund, neither company contributions nor accumulated interest being subject to tax.

Analysis of the tax-free investment approach indicates that since long-term governments issued after 1942 have generally been fully taxable, the investment would have to be in municipals. Aside from the question of their general representativeness, municipal bond rates had limited significance during the war years since there was little state and local government financing then. In the corporate trust fund approach, on the other hand, there is much to be said for employing high-grade corporate bonds as a compromise between low-interest, long-term governments and high-yield but risky common stock.

Using the corporate trust fund approach, the average interest rate on high-grade corporate bonds[2] was analyzed for the period 1900 to 1958, which spanned the corporate careers of the great majority of executives included in our study.[3] The rates, of course, varied from year to year. An argument can be made, in theory, that our present value calculations ought to reflect the variation. It is doubtful, however, whether the degree of accuracy of other estimates (for example, those on future values of stock) would justify the more involved computations. Accordingly, the approximate average interest rate for the whole period, 4 per cent, was selected instead.

How the rate of interest can be put to use is most easily understood by assuming that a man now invests some money at 4 per cent a year compound interest in a savings bank. He hopes to be able to take $100 out of the bank ten years hence and wants to know how much he must put into the bank now to get his $100 then. That sum, which works out to roughly $67.56, is the present value of $100. Or, we can say that $100 payable ten

2. Standard and Poor's *Security Price Index Record,* 1957 ed., p. 150, and 1959 supplement to 1957 ed., p. 20. Data are for yield to maturity of a composite of high-grade corporate bonds.

3. The reason for the relatively long time span will be clearer from the discussion of pensions in Chapter III.

years in the future is now worth only $67.56 (assuming interest at 4 per cent annually).

To demonstrate another version of present value, suppose a man would like to have $1,000 of extra income every year for the next ten years. How much money would he have to put in a savings bank now at 4 per cent interest to give him the extra $1,000 a year? This amount, which works out to $8,111, is the present value of $1,000 a year for ten years. Or, turning it around, we can say that an income of $1,000 a year over the next ten years is now worth $8,111, assuming interest at 4 per cent.

These two versions of present value apply directly to the problem of deferred bonuses. For instance, the case of a bonus payable in equal amounts over five years following the award is similar to that of the man who wants to have some extra yearly income. But figuring a bonus payable over the years after retirement uses both versions. First, we compute the present value of the series of postretirement payments at the year of retirement. Then we find the present worth at the year of the award of the value of the bonus at retirement, and this figure is also the present value at the year of the award of the postretirement payments.[4]

Unlike the problem of determining the present value of income payable in the future, the problems resulting from overlapping of income affect only the after-tax income values, and in no way concern the before-tax values of deferred bonuses. Overlapping of income occurs where in a given year an executive receives not only a salary but also parts of, say, five bonus awards made in different years. The significance of the overlapping lies in the fact that the executive pays a tax not on the separate layers of income but on the whole multilayered income sandwich. Therefore the effective tax rate applying to a single layer repre-

4. Present value tables in Justin H. Moore, *Handbook of Financial Mathematics* (New York: Prentice Hall, Inc., 1929), pp. 1068–1129, were used extensively. *Financial Handbook,* ed. Jules I. Bogen (New York: The Ronald Press Company, 1957), 3rd ed., pp. 1179, 1185, 1198, and 1205, contains identical tables.

senting, say, a single payment of a five-installment bonus will be the rate applying to the sandwich.

Since each income sandwich may comprise not only awards for years included in our sample but those for other past years and future years as well, it will often be necessary to estimate missing year bonus awards. We can obtain such estimates by using the ratio of bonus to salary for known years to develop the approximate percentage relationship of bonus to salary for different levels of salary. These percentage data will then be applied to salary data, derived from each executive's career salary curve, for the missing years in order to estimate the bonuses, whether they be short-term or postretirement, the simpler cash payment or the more complex payment in stock. A bonus paid in cash or stock over a period of several years immediately following the award—short-term deferment—was reported by six out of 39 firms in our sample of manufacturing companies during one or more years. Gulf Oil Corporation's cash bonus to one executive for the year 1958 provides a typical illustration of the problems involved in determining the value of short-term, cash-paid bonuses. The Gulf officer received a cash bonus of $90,000 and salary of $92,000.[5] The bonus was payable under the company's plan over a ten-year period at $9,000 per year. Before-tax value of the bonus, calculated as the present value of one dollar per year at 4 per cent for ten years, or $8.1109 times $9,000, was thus about $73,000. But finding the after-tax value of the 1958 bonus required a far more complex set of computations.

To get the after-tax value of the 1958 award, it was necessary to know the value of the awards for the years 1954, 1955, 1956, and 1957. Since the only known figure was for 1957, the other figures had to be estimated. Assuming retirement of the executive at the end of 1960, eight out of ten years of distribution of the 1958 award would be during the retirement period. But since 1956, 1957, 1959, and 1960 awards also overlap into the re-

5. Postretirement stock bonus is here disregarded for purposes of explanation.

tirement period, projection of future awards, for 1959 and 1960, was also required.

To estimate past awards, total amounts of incentive compensation awards were posted for each year from company annual reports going as far back as 1945.[6] From company and SEC records, amounts paid to officers, separately as to cash and stock, were determined for as many years as possible, with unknown years estimated by using the percentage relationship between the two series prevailing in adjacent years. Then a scatter diagram was made. On one axis was per cent of salary, for the one officer. On the other was the total cash awarded each year to all officers. Cash bonus as a per cent of salary was calculated for the two known years. Already known for the same years was the amount paid as cash bonus to all officers. This made it possible to plot a point for each of the two years. It was also assumed that a zero total award would mean a cash bonus of zero per cent of salary, which gave a point of origin. Using the three points, a rough line of relationship was drawn. It was then possible, for each year for which no award figures was available, to read off an estimated per cent of salary. This percentage was applied to the officer's salary to get an estimated award value.[7]

To get estimates of future cash bonuses for 1959 and 1960, the cash awards for 1952 to 1958 (including estimated awards) were totaled. Salary figures for the same years were added. Dividing total cash bonuses by total salaries, the result was 83 per cent. This was used against projected salary for 1959 and 1960.

After all the necessary award amounts had been calculated, they had to be spread over the years of payment. Under the Gulf Oil plan, payments to an executive close to retirement are stretched to reach more deeply into the retirement period, when taxes supposedly will be imposed on a lower level of income. This

6. For some companies, actual bonus awards to executives were obtained. Where even company totals for awards were not available, unknown past awards were related to information on company profits. The techniques followed here were applied also to postretirement bonuses.

7. For interpolation of past salary data and extrapolation of future salaries see Chapter I.

is done by providing that awards to officers less than sixty-three years of age at the end of the year are payable over five years while older executives are paid over a ten-year period.[8] For the executive in this example, the result was that the 1957 and earlier awards were distributable in five installments, while later awards were paid in ten installments.

For each taxable year, it was then necessary to total salary and the various pieces of bonuses in order to apply deductions and taxes. For 1959 (first year of payout of the 1958 bonus), we have a projected salary plus one installment from each of five different bonus awards, or a total adjusted gross income of $139,000. Applying deductions and taxes resulted in a tentative tax of $64,000 on 1959 income. Now, to spread the tax over the parts of the income, the share of each part compared to adjusted gross income was used. For example, the first installment of the 1958 award, payable in 1959, was 6.5 per cent of the 1959 adjusted gross income. Using this percentage against the tentative tax for 1959 resulted in a tax on the 1959 installment of $4.2 thousand, leaving an after-tax net for this installment of $9.0 thousand minus $4.2 thousand or $4.8 thousand. For 1961 and later years which overlap the retirement period, the procedure was similar except that adjusted gross income and taxes were taken from the retirement income schedule, which reflected other elements such as pension and postretirement stock as well as cash bonus installments.

The foregoing process resulted in a series of unequal after-tax installments from the 1958 award. So the present value of each installment was figured separately and these values were totaled. This gave an after-tax income value of $56,000 for the 1958 bonus award.

Turning now to bonuses paid in stock, Chrysler Corporation's stock bonus provides a typical illustration of the measurement problems arising in connection with this kind of deferred bonus. The differences in measuring stock and cash are of two kinds—

8. Proxy statement, March 23, 1954.

one purely incidental to the company,[9] the other having to do with the added complications resulting from stock. Except for such differences, the procedures of measurement are the same as in the earlier example of cash payments.[10]

Regardless of whether one is dealing with award values of stock or values at the time shares are received, it is necessary to convert all shares to a common basis to take into account stock splits and dividends.[11] This has been done here and elsewhere in the study by converting shares and prices to the basis of the latest reported bonus award. This meant, in general, a scaling down of price per share and an increase in the number of shares for earlier years, in such a way that dollar values remained the same. A similar type of adjustment was made for dividends.

For estimating awards for missing years, stock was taken at its value at the time of the award. At the time of distribution, however, all shares are fungible. A share from one award is worth no more nor less than that from another award. Therefore, shares when distributed were taken at yearly average market value[12] at the year of distribution. Future shares were taken at 1958 prices, no attempt being made to forecast future stock prices.

Dividends were included in income for any shares of stock not yet in the physical possession of the executive, on the basis that this type of dividend payment is more of a payment by the corporation for the executive's services than it is a purely investment proposition. The inclusion of dividends made a change

9. For earlier years, this involved conversion of SEC bonus information based on receipts back to an award year basis.

10. Bonuses for recent years for Du Pont and GM include income values of dividend units and contingent credits on the basis of options not being exercised. For both companies bonus calculations reflected option grants made up through 1958 only.

11. This applies whether stock is delivered over the years following the award or deferred after retirement, but of course more so in the latter case, as more splits and stock dividends are likely to have taken place over the longer time span. As an example of these complications, Gulf Oil paid stock dividends after cash over the five-year period 1954 through 1958 of 4 per cent, 4 per cent, 5 per cent, 5 per cent, and 4 per cent.

12. Average of high and low for the year.

32

in the after-tax income of the executives receiving bonuses. While cash and stock (when distributed as a bonus) are taxable on the same basis, dividends are subject to the special provisions of the Internal Revenue Code of 1954. To reflect this, the share of tentative tax applied to each bonus installment was reduced for 1954 and later years by a tax credit equal to 4 per cent of the dividends included in the installment.

Bonuses paid during the years following an executive's retirement were reported in one year or another by eight of the 39 firms included in the study sample. As was pointed out earlier, the problem of measuring postretirement deferred bonuses is a two-phase one, requiring a determination of the present value at the year of retirement of the postretirement payments, and then the determination at the year of award of the present value of the retirement year amount.

Aluminum Corporation of America provides a typical case of cash payment of postretirement bonuses. Taking one executive appearing in recent years, missing awards had to be obtained for the years from 1953 through 1961, the expected year of retirement. Total awards were roughly $400,000, which, divided by the five years over which distributed, yielded $80,000 per year. This plus a noncontributory pension of $38,000 resulted in adjusted gross income of $118,000 for the first five years, dropping afterwards to the level of the pension for the remaining years of expected life. After the usual application of deductions and taxes, and the split between pension and bonus, cash payments after taxes amounted to around $45,000 for each of the installments. The present value of all five payments at the end of 1961 (year of retirement) was roughly $356,000 before, $200,000 after taxes. Taking 1957, 12 per cent of the $200,000 after taxes, or $24,000, was considered to belong to 1957. But since retirement was four years away, the $24,000 was multiplied by $.8548 (the present value of one dollar over four years) to give a final after-tax income value of slightly over $20,000.

The instance of a Texaco executive can be used to illustrate a postretirement bonus paid in stock as distinct from cash. The

33

measurement aspects of stock compared to cash, which were considered in the case of stock bonuses payable over the years immediately following the award, apply with even greater force to the present instance. For example, as to appreciation of stock values, the Texaco officer received some shares awarded in 1950 when the price was around $17.37 (adjusted for splits, and so on) per share, and other shares awarded in 1958, when the price was around $71.88, or four times the 1950 figure. Room for such appreciation in value is typically far greater where stock is distributed after retirement rather than over the years following the award. Yet, for assessment of taxes, all shares distributed at the same time had to be valued equally. There are also other measurement features in postretirement stock bonuses not present in the case of such bonuses in cash. These include such matters as the accumulation of shares of stock, pre- and postretirement dividends, and the method used for split-down of present values at the year of retirement back to award years.

The fact that cumulative shares of stock awarded are included in proxy statements makes it possible to estimate missing past year awards with greater accuracy than was the case for cash awards. For Texaco, scatter diagrams were used in order to get tentative award values for each of the missing past years. Per share prices were divided into the awards to get a tentative number of shares for each year. By totaling the tentative shares and comparing this with the actual accumulated shares, a factor was derived which was used to scale down the final number of shares for each year. This meant in one year, for example, that a tentative award of 481 shares was reduced to 252 shares.

On postretirement stock, there are normally two types of dividends, which we can call preretirement and postretirement dividends. Preretirement dividends are those which accumulate on shares awarded and not yet distributed during the years before retirement.[13] Postretirement dividends are those which accumulate after retirement on shares not yet distributed. For the

13. These are not paid as they accumulate partly because they would presumably be taxable to the recipient at a higher rate if paid currently.

3 4

Texaco officer, the preretirement dividends, including future dividends projected using the 1958 dividend rate, were estimated at about $420,000, assumed to be distributed at $42,000 a year along with the stock. Postretirement dividends valued at the 1958 dividend rate showed a different pattern. The first installment of 1,617 shares of stock carried with it $3,800 in postretirement dividends while such dividends in the tenth year were estimated at $38,000. This came about because dividends accumulated and were paid out along with the matching stock. Thus, the first installment of stock had attached to it one year's dividends, while the tenth installment had ten years of dividends with it.[14]

The distribution to award years of the present value of the stock, before and after taxes, at the year of retirement was based on shares of stock awarded, rather than on amounts of cash awarded, as was the case for cash bonuses.

Both electrical companies in the 25-company sample have plans which show variations from the standard pattern of postretirement stock bonuses. Westinghouse has a plan that provides that dividends accumulating on the stock, both before and after retirement, be converted into more shares of stock. This made for a simpler set of calculations for this company. The GE calculations were somewhat more complex than for other companies having deferred stock bonus plans because of the attention given by the company to relating the period of years over which installments were to be paid to the age and life expectancy of executives. While for the most part such companies had a flat five- or ten-year payout period, the GE plan varied the number of installments with age at retirement. The period of payout went through one major change in the earlier fifties: from payout over a ten-to-fifteen-year period to payout over a fifteen-to-twenty-year period, depending on the executive's age.[15]

14. Actually all installments of stock pay out equal amounts of dividends, but dividends paid on stock already in the physical possession of the executive are not counted in the total since these dividends, of course, lie outside our income concept.

15. Sources: Form 10-K, 1958, and proxy statement, April 20, 1948.

Trends in Bonuses, 1929–1958

Let us look now at what the concepts of measurement show when they are applied to the 25-company sample over the period 1929–1958 for the spot years for which measurements were taken. First a word of caution on the limitations of the data. Interpretation of trends shown in the diagrams to follow should be made with the limitations of the data in mind. Among these are the results of the $30,000 reporting rule under SEC Regulations, and possible undervaluation of stock bonus benefits due to appreciation in the price of the stock.

From the analysis of earlier SEC reporting requirements, it appears that, at least from 1935 through 1946, companies were not required to report bonuses separately for each executive, unless they were in excess of $30,000 in each case. Some companies have followed a practice of rotating bonuses so that not all of the top three will show a bonus for a given year. On the other hand, it is apparent that, for many firms, bonuses were often less than $30,000 and hence did not have to be reported. In one or two concerns where an examination of the data strongly suggested that such bonuses existed, estimates were made and probable amounts, usually based on a percentage of salary consistent with other top officers, were separated out from aggregate remuneration shown in the SEC totals. Still, it seems likely that in the 1935–1946 period, there may be some understatement of the amounts of bonuses. This probably means that salaries have been correspondingly overstated, and bonus data for 1929 may also be understated in connection with management trusts.

While this study includes no forecasts of price appreciation of stock, it would be naïve to pretend that the managements of the largest companies did not evolve their stock bonus plans with this feature in mind. Wilford J. Eiteman and Frank P. Smith, in a study of stock prices over the 55-year period 1897 to 1951, concluded that, despite cyclical changes, stocks have moved upward in price at an average annual rate of 3.19 per cent.[16] It may well be that the stock prices of the 25 largest manufacturing companies in the present study would, if taken as a composite, show a more pronounced upward trend. In any case, the writer has determined to his own satisfaction that one out of the 25 companies uses in its forecasting an assumption of a 5 per cent a year climb in the price of its stock. Thus, bonuses, to the extent paid in stock, could turn out to be seriously understated.

It is possible that, in the diagrams for certain of the early years, some bonuses may have been misclassified as to type of bonus due to lack of adequate information. In general, classifications were not changed because of temporary changes in plans. GM and Du Pont, in several of the World War II years, paid current cash bonuses instead of deferred stock payable over the years following the award. In particular, the 1942 data for short-term deferment are overstated, and current bonuses understated by the amounts of the GM payments.[17]

The four diagrams in this chapter are designed to show both growth rates and changes in the percentage makeup of the bonus part of the top executive pay package. All the data include the three top officers taken together and are for all of the 25 companies in the sample for each year measured.

In the first two diagrams, a semilogarithmic grid is used so that differing rates of growth can be judged by comparing the slopes

16. Wilford J. Eiteman and Frank P. Smith, "Common Stock Values and Yields," *Michigan Business Studies*, XI, No. 3 (June, 1953), p. 7.

17. Aside from the cautions mentioned here, bonus data reflect minor differences in reporting by individual companies. For example, GE, in its report for the year 1957, included in one figure "salaries and approximately half of the incentive compensation awarded in 1957 for services rendered in 1956." This portion of incentive compensation was stated to be in cash, with shares of stock shown separately. Du Pont, in its report to SEC for 1948, identified salaries and fees for 1948 and the Class B Bonus Award "for the year 1948. No amount of bonuses awarded for earlier years but delivered or made available to officers in 1948 is included." Such differences as these probably are not too important to those looking for trends, but might be of concern for the student of year-to-year or cyclical changes.

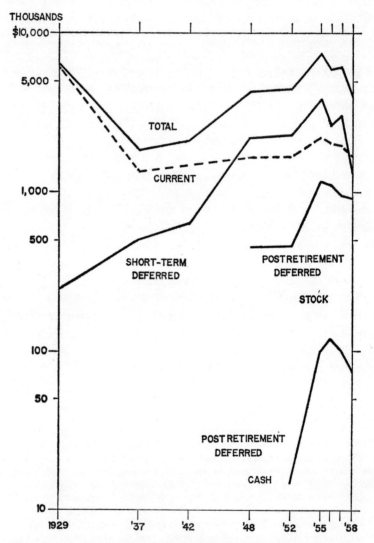

THOUSANDS
$10,000

5,000

TOTAL

CURRENT

1,000

500

SHORT-TERM DEFERRED

POST RETIREMENT DEFERRED

STOCK

100

50

POST RETIREMENT DEFERRED

CASH

10

1929   '37   '42   '48   '52   '55   '58

Diagram 4—Bonus Trends Before Taxes, Top Three Together

3 8

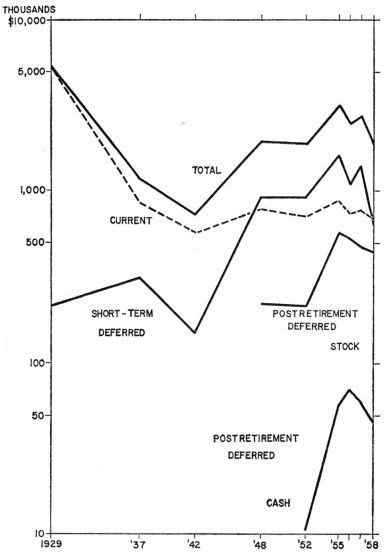

THOUSANDS

$10,000

5,000

TOTAL

1,000

CURRENT

500

SHORT - TERM

DEFERRED

POST RETIREMENT
DEFERRED

STOCK

100

50

POST RETIREMENT

DEFERRED

CASH

10

1929   '37   '42   '48   '52 '55 '58

Diagram 5—Bonus Trends After Taxes, Top Three Together

39

of the lines. The steeper the slope, the faster the rate of growth. From Diagrams 4 and 5 we see that bonuses in general dropped sharply after 1929, and, if looked at after taxes, did not reach bottom until 1942. Moreover, bonuses appear to have recovered after World War II, but, if we allow for taxes, they did not return to the high level of 1929. Most of the initial drop in 1929 was caused by the decline in current cash and stock bonuses. The decline appears to be both substantial and permanent, with only meager evidence of recent revival. Bonuses deferred over the years following the award (short-term deferred) have been growing, with some variation, since 1929—a longer-term movement than is perhaps generally realized. After taxes, short-term deferred bonuses dived in 1942, but other types of bonuses also dropped because wartime taxes were effective. Recent peaks and valleys in short-term deferred bonuses, on the other hand, reflect largely the profit picture. Postretirement deferred bonuses, mostly in stock, are of more recent origin, and have increased sharply, especially since 1952.

Diagrams 6 and 7 show what share each type of bonus—current, short-term deferred, and postretirement deferred—is of the total for all bonuses. Changes in these shares over the years are shown. Allowing for the unusual nature of the 1942 tax picture, the more significant facts emerge from the after-tax view shown in Diagram 7: current bonuses dropped from 96 per cent of the total in 1929 to less than 38 per cent in 1958; postretirement bonuses have risen from nowhere to account for over a quarter of the bonus part of the pay package; short-term deferred bonuses have risen from only 4 per cent to constitute well over a third of the bonus total.

The Size of the Bonus

When bonuses are discussed, some people are apt to point to their value as an incentive, while others are prone to argue that

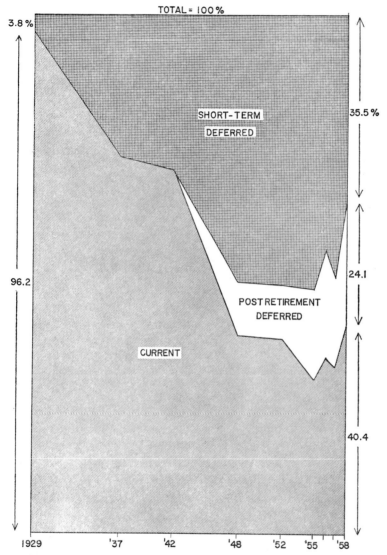

Diagram 6—Bonus Package Before Taxes, Top Three Together

41

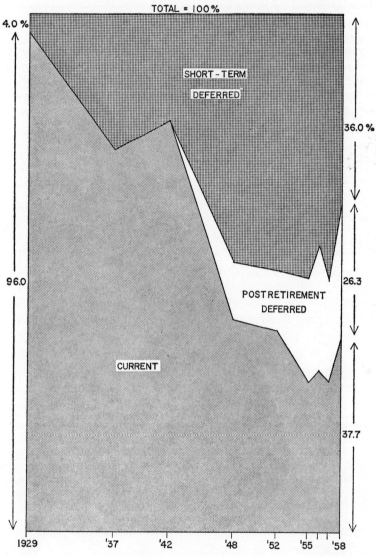

TOTAL = 100%

4.0 %

SHORT – TERM
DEFERRED

36.0 %

96.0

POST RETIREMENT
DEFERRED

26.3

CURRENT

37.7

1929   '37   '42   '48   '52   '55   '58

Diagram 7—Bonus Package After Taxes, Top Three Together

42

the bonuses paid are too big. This raises the question of how large a bonus ought to be. When is it inadequate? When is it excessive? Although these questions are more easily raised than answered, it is possible to consider bonuses in relation to standards such as salary,[18] the stockholder's dividend, and company earnings.

With respect to the relation of bonuses to salary, Richard C. Smyth has expressed the view that a bonus opportunity of 20 per cent of salary is the minimum that will be "effective on a sustained basis as an incentive at any level of management position."[19] He goes on to add, however, assuming base salaries are paid at the going rate, that for top-level positions the plan should provide for "a bonus opportunity of 40% to 60% of base salary for outstanding personal performance in a year when the company makes a good fiscal showing."[20]

In the light of the above standards, it is interesting to see what the present study reveals concerning the 11 out of 25 companies which paid bonuses to their top three officers in 1958. The results are shown in Table 4. From the table we may observe that bonuses paid to Bethlehem Steel's top three are far in excess of the 40 per cent to 60 per cent standard thought necessary to provide adequate incentive, even making allowance for the somewhat lower level of salaries compared to other firms on the list. But in view of the lower salaries, it appears that some part of the bonus could really be regarded, not as an incentive bonus at all, but as a substitute for salary. For the

18. Salary will be used as a standard here in judging the size of the bonus. The relation of bonuses to the total pay package is not considered as significant, since the various types of bonuses from an economic viewpoint are nonhomogeneous. Their differences are more important than their similarities. However, the present study does show that total bonuses before taxes in 1929 were 52 per cent of the total pay package for the top three executives in the 25 largest companies. For other years, the figure was in the 20 per cent to 25 per cent range, without visible trend.

19. Richard C. Smyth, "Bonus Plans for Executives," *Harvard Business Review*, XXXVII, No. 4 (1959), p. 68.

20. *Ibid.* Setting of the rate at 40 per cent to 60 per cent presumably makes some allowance for the higher level of taxes affecting executive incomes.

next five companies shown, salaries appear in line with those for the other firms. Again, however, bonuses are distinctly generous in comparison to the indicated percentage standard.

Table 4—Bonuses as Per Cent of Salaries
Three Highest Paid Executives, 1958
(Dollars in Thousands)

Company	Salaries	Bonuses[a]	Per Cent
Bethlehem Steel	$250	$1,049	420
General Electric	390	532	136
General Motors	476	617	130
Gulf Oil	392	448	114
Du Pont	441	498	113
International Business Machines	367	392	107
Westinghouse Electric	379	138	37
Goodyear Tire and Rubber	444	157	35
The Texas Company	423	135	32
Aluminum Company of America	372	77	21
International Harvester	244	28	12

[a] Currently paid bonuses are actual. Others are income values.

The five companies at the bottom of the list, on the contrary, awarded bonuses for 1958 which failed to meet the 40 per cent minimum needed to provide an adequate incentive. While the bonuses paid by some of these companies doubtlessly result from a less favorable financial showing, it can be argued that if these bonuses provided inadequate incentive it would have been better to have forgone them in 1958. Two companies not in the table but in the top 25 and having bonus plans—Chrysler and Ford—did in fact forgo bonuses to their top three in 1958.

The stockholder's dividend has been at stake in some of the many disputes over the size of bonuses. The bonus plans of American Tobacco, Bethlehem Steel, and General Motors have all been before the courts in connection with stockholder suits. Compared to the other firms, however, Bethlehem Steel's bonus plan has been much more in the public eye, having been in and out of the courts for a period of almost three decades.

In 1931, when as a result of the Youngstown merger suit, details of Bethlehem's bonus plan came to light, a stockholders protective committee was formed and searing letters pointed to

44

such alleged facts as these: details of the bonus system had been kept from stockholders' knowledge until the merger suit; bonuses up to the end of 1928 were about 80 per cent of the amount paid out to stockholders; in 1925–1928 stockholders got nothing, but $6.8 million was paid out as bonuses; an 8 per cent maximum limit on bonuses in the by-laws had been exceeded (this point was highly technical and was contested by the company); bonuses went only to a handful of favored directors and other executives; over $1.5 million in 1929 and $1 million in 1930 were paid to the president in bonuses, even though the company failed to earn its dividends in the latter year.[21] Following the settlement of the 1931 litigation, according to Baker,[22] a provision in the bonus plan stated that total executive bonus payments should be reported annually to the stockholders.

The New York State Supreme Court in 1941 entered a judgment "in favor of Bethlehem Steel." The court decided, however, that the individual defendants in prior actions should have made a part of the payments made by the corporation in settlement of the actions, the total being the amount of the judgment, exclusive of interest. The net credit to surplus resulting from amounts payable by certain officers and directors was roughly $640,000.[23]

Finally, a more recent stockholder suit, started in 1957, again sought an accounting of bonuses, alleging overpayment. The suit had the effect of delaying a changeover in the Bethlehem plan from a cash bonus to the payment of dividend units. The final settlement in 1959 allowed the new pay plan to go through, but involved a limit on total compensation to executives which was to be at least 11 per cent below the level then prevailing.[24]

Such experience with stockholders' suits, together with the

21. Letters to stockholders of Bethlehem Steel from Protective Committee for Stockholders of Bethlehem Steel Corporation, dated March 20, and April 29, 1931.
22. John C. Baker, *op. cit.*, p. 207.
23. Company annual report for 1941.
24. *The New York Times,* August 26 and September 17, 1959.

enactment of the Securities Act of 1933 and the Securities Exchange Act of 1934, have made many of the largest companies more circumspect than formerly with regard to the treatment of the stockholder. These companies no longer feel free to pay out large bonuses when they omit to pay dividends,[25] and newly installed bonus plans or changes in plans are usually submitted to stockholders for approval before going into effect. Many plans, too, now relate bonuses to earnings by formulas which provide some protection to stockholders.[26] For example, the General Motors plan allows as a credit for bonuses (and stock options) an amount of up to "12% of the net earnings after deducting 5% on net capital, but not in excess of the amount paid out as dividends on the common stock of the corporation during that year."[27]

Relating of bonuses to company profits by a formula such as that shown above prevents the amounts given out as bonuses from being completely arbitrary. An exclusion—such as the 5 per cent in the quotation—gives the company financial protection in meeting the minimum capital requirements needed for growth. The percentage used against the balance to determine the maximum bonus amount for the year—12 per cent for General Motors—serves as a further limit. Yet under the formula indicated, General Motors in the peak profits year of 1955 still could provide a credit to the bonus fund of $95 million.[28]

One approach to whether this amount may have been excessive is to consider alternative uses of the money. If given to the stockholders, it appears that no more than 16 cents per share

25. Nor do they tend to lean to the opposite extreme and distribute bonuses in proportion to employee stockholdings, instead of either salary or performance. R. J. Reynolds Tobacco used to do this under a plan no longer in effect. For the years in the present study which reflected this plan, special estimates of the bonus amounts were made on the basis of the yearly bonus provision, individual stockholdings, etc.

26. Nicholas L. A. Martucci, "Computing the Executive Bonus Fund," *Management Record* (October, 1955), pp. 390–393.

27. Company annual report, 1958.

28. *Ibid.*

46

would have been added to the $2.17 received that year.[29] If passed on to the consumer in the form of a price concession it would have meant a reduction of less than 1 per cent. On the other hand, if the amount had been distributed equally to all wage and salary employees it would have meant an increase for each employee of $152 a year, or if figured as a share of payroll, about 3 per cent of pay for each employee.[30]

Keeping in mind that all the figures cited above are for a peak year, and assuming that only the excess over the amount considered necessary as incentives for higher-ranking executives was used for other than bonuses, then all the gains cited for alternative uses of the money would be correspondingly smaller. Thus we can conclude that while present bonuses at General Motors may be unduly generous, redistribution of the excess to others, those farther down the organizational ladder, for example, would not result in bonanzas of the dimensions sometimes envisioned.

While most of the bonus plans of the largest manufacturers are based on profits, another method of relating reward to individual performance is illustrated by Du Pont's Plan A Bonus. Du Pont grants such awards for "conspicuous service regardless of company earnings."[31] These awards contrast with Class B awards which have been granted generally to members of management only.[32] Apparently, however, Class A awards are sometimes given to top executives, for one of the top three officers of the company received such an award in 1948.[33] In a report to

29. The 16 cents assumes the whole amount is paid out as dividends, thus doubling the amount of 8 cents in Smyth, *op. cit.*, p. 67.

30. Calculated from company annual report, 1958.

31. J. K. Lasser and V. Henry Rothschild, "Deferred Compensation for Executives," *Harvard Business Review*, XXXIII, No. 1 (January–February, 1955), 92.

32. Class B awards are made "to those who in a general way contribute to the company's success . . . including those who have proven themselves qualified to occupy important managerial posts and to succeed to higher positions." Current Report to SEC, Form 8-K, May 15, 1944.

33. The proxy statement did not identify the amount but included it with this officer's aggregate remuneration.

the SEC in 1936, the company described Class A awards as follows:

Class A awards concerning a specific money-saving device or invention are made over a 5-year period in 3 parts roughly after the end of the first, third, and fifth years. However the first award may be in as short a period as 6 months, the period depending on the time needed to demonstrate the practicality of the scheme. If after the third year it looks as if the savings were strictly limited, the executive committee may treat the award as a two-part award and make the final award.[34]

34. Current Report to SEC, Form 8-K, December, 1936.

III

Postretirement
Benefits

Postretirement bonuses have certain traits in common with short-term deferred bonuses. For example, both devices allow for spreading income over the years of payout, and both schemes are commonly thought to have a strong tendency to hold the executive with the company. It is generally felt, however, that postretirement payment—whether in the form of a bonus, deferred cash payments under contract, or pension—has certain distinct characteristics. For one thing, there is, in the case of bonuses, a greater lapse of time between award and payment. Another, more general, point is that deferring payment until after retirement may result in lower taxes, with income presumably at a lower level or subject to capital gains treatment. Finally, it is often stated that the holding effect on the executive of postretirement payment is greater since the executive must remain with the firm until he reaches retirement in order to gain the full benefit.

In this chapter, we shall explore the determination of income values for postretirement benefits and analyze the trends. We shall also discuss the retirement age of top executives.

Income Values of Deferred Cash Payments and Pensions

In the previous chapter we saw that finding the income value of a postretirement deferred bonus was a two-phase problem. One phase involved determining the value at the year of retirement of the postretirement payments. In this phase, there is no essential difference between the computations for a deferred cash bonus on the one hand, and those for deferred cash under contract or a pension[1] on the other. However, the similarity ends here, since in the second phase they are altogether different.

In the case of the postretirement bonus, awards were typically repeated each year, and we could relate the benefit back to a particular award year. Deferred cash payments under contract and pension benefits have more of a one-shot nature, and yet they differ from a single bonus award in that the benefit is related, not to a single year, but to a period of years during which the executive is protected by the contract or is accruing pension credits. The problem will be to relate the retirement year amount back to this period of years.

In relating the retirement year value of deferred cash payments under contract back to the years during which the officer is protected by the contract, it could be argued that the income value of the contract in any year would be the fixed amount which the executive would otherwise have to contribute (assuming interest at 4 per cent on the money) each year in order to buy the postretirement benefits. If, however, the contract protection extended over many years, an executive in his earlier years when he earned less might have to contribute an amount

1. There are certain other differences, however, in the case of a pension, which will be explained later.

50

regarded by him as too heavy a burden. But in successful years closer to retirement, he might feel that he could easily contribute a much larger amount.

There is, of course, an easy way out of this particular dilemma. We can think of the income value of the deferred cash payments as being the share of his pay an executive would otherwise have to set aside each year to buy the postretirement benefits. The money is assumed to be placed in a corporate trust fund, the interest on the money being tax free while it accumulates. Suppose the share of pay worked out to 5 per cent of salary. Then if the executive's salary were $100,000 for a given year, the value of his benefits for that year, before taxes, would be $5,000.

We have assumed above a certain percentage of salary. We did so merely to indicate the desired result. The percentage, in fact, is not actually known and will have to be computed. The problem is to spread the value at retirement of the pay-out over the career salary curve of the executive for the period of the pay-in, a fixed percentage of the executive's pay being set aside each year. We shall also have to take into account the fact that each amount set aside will accumulate interest. This type of problem can be resolved by means of a mathematical device, which we shall call the *equivalent key*. Its use is illustrated in Table 5.

Table 5—The Equivalent Key

Years	Periods	Salary[a]	Fraction Set Aside	Amount[b] of $1 at 4 Per Cent	Amount Set Aside at Interest[a]
1948	4	$50	X	$1.1699	$58.495X
1949	3	60	X	1.1249	67.494X
1950	2	70	X	1.0816	75.712X
1951	1	80	X	1.0400	83.200X
1952	0	90	X	1.0000	90.000X
Total					$374.901X[a]

[a] Thousands. The $374.901 is the equivalent key.
[b] *Financial Handbook,* p. 1179, or Moore, op. cit., p. 1076.

Table 5 shows the derivation of the equivalent key for a hypothetical case, that of an executive who retired at the end of 1952. It is assumed that he will receive a series of payments during retirement (deferred cash under contract, or pension) whose present value at the end of 1952, assuming interest at 4 per cent, was estimated to be $85 thousand before taxes. We also assumed that the period of pay-in was 1948 through 1952. The problem then is to find the value of the unknown X, the fraction of salary which would have had to be set aside at the end of each year of pay-in, in order to buy the postretirement benefits, again assuming amounts set aside earned interest at 4 per cent.

For an example, take the line in the table for 1952. Out of an assumed $90 thousand of salary, the officer set aside a fraction, X. Since this was paid at the end of 1952, when the executive retired, no interest had accumulated on the sum and the amount of the set-aside for 1952 at interest was $90.000X$ thousand, as shown in the last column.

Now let us look at the first line of the table. At the end of 1948, the officer contributed out of his $50 thousand salary another fraction, also X. The amount set aside accumulated interest at 4 per cent for four periods (1952 minus 1948). The product of one dollar at 4 per cent for four periods is $1.1699. This, multiplied by the amount of the set-aside, $50X$ thousand, resulted in $58.495X$ thousand, again as shown in the last column.

Totaling all the set-asides at interest, which appear in the last column, yields $374.901X$ thousand. This is another way of expressing the value of the retirement income at the end of the year of retirement, which was originally estimated to be worth $85 thousand. Therefore we can say, using rough thousands, that $375X = \$85$ or $X = .23$, approximately. This fraction applied to the salary for any given year yields the income value of the benefit for that year.

The $375 thousand (or more accurately $374.901 thousand) is the *equivalent key* in this case.[2] The equivalent key can be de-

2. The equivalent key will be different for each case. A careful examination of the table will make clear that by employing a standard strip (with from zero to 50 periods, say) showing the amounts of one dollar at 4 per cent, we can multiply the figures on the strip by the figures in any salary curve, using the cumulative multiplication features of the latest calculating machines, and thus compute the equivalent key.

52

fined as that figure, which, multiplied by the unknown fraction of salary, X, is equal to the present value of postretirement payments at the end of the year of retirement.

A typical example of deferred cash payments is provided in the case of U.S. Steel. Deferred fixed cash payments under contract were arranged for three officers of the corporation after World War II.[3] The contracts provided for deferred compensation after retirement for the rest of their lives in an amount per year determined by multiplying $5 thousand by the years of service after May 6, 1941, but limited to a maximum of $50 thousand. This was afterwards liberalized so that each officer would receive more than the earlier specified maximum.[4] One of the three officers was scheduled to receive $70 thousand. To avoid complexities of measurement, we shall consider what he will finally get and not the interim amount.[5] We can break the problem down into two parts: the determination of the value, first of the pay-out, and then of the pay-in.

The pay-out was determined in general by methods considered earlier.[6] The retirement income schedule for this executive included the taxable portion of a pension, as well as deferred cash payments. Together, the two items made up the adjusted gross income. After the usual calculations and splitting of tax between the two pay items, the present value at the end of the year of retirement of the postretirement cash payments was found. This worked out to roughly $778 thousand before taxes, $463 thousand afterwards.

The problem of the pay-in was to relate the retirement year values back to the executive's career salary curve. After estimating the salary curve, the equivalent key was computed. This worked out to about $2,754 thousand. The two present values, shown above, at the year of retirement were divided by the equivalent key to yield .283 and .168. Finally these two frac-

3. Proxy statement, April 1, 1946.
4. Annual Report to SEC, Form 10-K, 1951.
5. This will be discussed at greater length in connection with pensions.
6. See Chapter II, p. 28.

tions were applied against salary for each year in which we were interested. For the year 1948 the income values of the deferred cash payments worked out to about $57 thousand before taxes, $34 thousand after taxes.[7]

The problem of measuring the income value of future pension benefits is conceptually similar to that of deferred cash payments under contract, although there are some differences. A pension is tailored to the individual's career salary curve, length of service with company, and age at retirement. Pensions, moreover, are often contributory, so that part of the benefit is really just a return of contributions, and pensions are also subject to special tax treatment.

The major difference in considering pensions, however, lies in the nature of the pay-in period. To illustrate the difference, we shall consider two different types of situations, one of a company having a plan whose benefits over a period of time are liberalized, the other of a company with a pension plan just recently installed.

The situation of a company having liberalized benefits is a fairly typical one for many of the 25 largest manufacturing concerns. Let us assume that a company has a plan which went into effect in 1915. An executive joins the company in 1925 and retires in 1958. For the purpose of argument we assume that the shape of the executive's career salary curve is not altered, that we know it in advance. Now under successive changes in the plan this executive would receive perhaps $10,000 a year under the

7. In certain instances, it was hard to distinguish between deferred cash payments under contract and pensions. An example is provided by the early contracts covering two officers of Republic Steel. In the present study, because of the details relating the benefits to past and future years of service (Annual Report to SEC, Form 10-K, 1939, Exhibit F-6.), these benefits were included under pensions. In the case of Dow Chemical, profit-sharing benefits tied in with a pension plan are included in the deferred bonus totals. Nevertheless, the method of computation used was the same as for deferred cash payments under contract. The 6½ per cent of salary limit on profit-sharing cited in Financial Notes to Annual Report to SEC, Form 10-K, 1959, was used in this connection. On the other hand, an Anaconda Copper contract applying to one officer, while included in the totals for deferred cash under contract, seemed to partake somewhat of a deferred bonus payable in cash, and so was valued using the method described in Chapter II.

plan as originally set up, $20,000 in 1945 after the first liberalization, $40,000 in 1950 when the plan was again made more generous, and now in 1955, after another upward adjustment, $60,000. To find the income value of his pension for the year 1955, we ought in strict theory to figure that what the executive gets is not $60,000 a year with a pay-in period of 33 years (1958 minus 1925), but really $10,000, paid in for over 33 years; another $10,000 ($20,000 minus $10,000), paid in for over 13 years (1958 minus 1945); still an added $20,000 resulting from the 1950 hike and bought over 8 years and finally a last $20,000 resulting from the 1955 liberalization to be financed in effect over a three-year period. To do all this would require the computation of four pay-in periods, four equivalent keys, and so forth.

It is clear that measurement of income values of pensions in such detail is too cumbersome to be useful. A practical modification of the pure concept to overcome the difficulty is to use a single pay-in and to base calculations on the benefit that is actually received or the executive expects to receive under the latest plan.[8]

Another type of situation worth exploring is that in which a company has only recently installed a pension plan. To this kind of situation we can bring three different approaches. One is to spread the period of pay-in over the years an executive participates in the plan. A second way is to use plan years, but to include only future service benefits in computing the value of the pension. A third approach is to spread the pay-in over the years of service.

Using the plan year approach, let us assume that a company has

8. This results in some overstatement of pensions in earlier years where, for example, we would be showing an executive with a pension income value in 1937 based on the more generous plan he actually retired under in 1952. To this extent we anticipate the benefit. The overstatement for the early years is compensated for by two facts. First, many executives listed among the three highest in 1937 and other years were no longer around in 1952, and did in fact retire under earlier, less liberal plans. Second, many of those who were around were being paid less, so that with income values related to the salary curve, the amount of the income value is lower than it would be for later years even under the same plan.

a plan starting in 1955. The company would be showing heavy income values in the early years of the plan, such as 1956, 1957, and 1958, for executives retiring in those years, compared to similar executives in other concerns whose plans started earlier. This results from the contrasting pay-in periods—say two years against thirty years. Under the plan year approach, a firm whose plan started as early as 1904 would show smaller income values for an executive having exactly the same length of service, career salary curve, and retirement age, even if he retired under an identical pension formula. In short, one disadvantage is a company-to-company bias.

In addition, with most pension plans coming into existence during the World War II years or shortly thereafter, there would be a big historical bump in the aggregates. When companies first put in plans, the swollen income values of early retirees increase the totals. Aggregates for earlier years including fewer companies would be smaller. But the aggregates for the later years would also be reduced because of the gradual lengthening of the pay-in period and the shrinking of the abnormally swollen income values, despite the fact that pension benefits were actually increasing. This latter tendency would, of course, eventually overcome the former, but a false trend might result in the interim.

A possible remedy to the weakness of the method of using plan years for the pay-in period might be to use plan years but to try to offset this by including only future service benefits in the pension amounts. For analyzing this proposition, we use two executives, Mr. A and Mr. B, in two different companies. Each started working for his employer in 1930 and planned to retire in 1958 on a pension of $50,000. The career salary curves of each are assumed to be as follows:

(In thousands of dollars)

1941	12	1947	30	1953	60
1942	15	1948	33	1954	70
1943	18	1949	36	1955	80
1944	21	1950	40	1956	90
1945	24	1951	45	1957	100
1946	27	1952	50	1958	110

There is only one difference between Mr. A and Mr. B. Mr. A's firm started its plan with future service dating from 1940, while Mr. B's concern did not do so until 1955. Table 6 compares their situations.

Table 6—Future Service Benefits of Two Executives in Different Companies
(In thousands of dollars)

	Past	SERVICE Future	Total	Future Service Benefit[a]	Assumed Present Value at Retirement[b]
Mr. A	10	18	28	$32.2	$322
Mr. B	25	3	28	$ 5.4	$ 54

[a] Assumes each year of past and future service is valued equally.
[b] Equal pay-out periods assumed.

From the table it can be seen that for Mr. A the larger future service benefit is spread over a longer period of pay-in, while Mr. B's smaller future service benefit is spread over a shorter period of pay-in. The hypothesis was that the two income values would about balance each other. The actual results, however, based on the assumptions we have used, indicate that the inclusion of only future service benefits while retaining the idea of plan years still leaves a company-to-company bias (see Table 7).

Table 7—Income Values of Future Service Benefits
(In thousands of dollars)

	Mr. A	Mr. B
Equivalent key	$1,083	$311
Present value at retirement	$ 322	$ 54
Fraction of salary	.297	.174
1956 income value	$ 26.7	$ 15.7

Another equally important point is that this approach omits from inclusion in the income values received by corporate executives enormous sums of money in the form of past service pension benefits, which have a substantial effect on both postretirement income and the tax rates applying against such income.

Thus our third possible approach, spreading pay-in over the years of service instead of over plan years (regardless of how future service benefits are handled), has certain advantages. It accurately reflects the peculiar nature of pension benefits, which are in reality more closely related to both pay and service than to other factors. In a real sense a pension is a reward for service. The years of service approach avoids both weaknesses cited in the other two approaches. There is neither distortion of company-to-company comparisons nor serious distortion of aggregates.

A disadvantage of a pay-in spread over the years of service is that in theory one would show income values for years when no plan existed. On the other hand, this can be handled by regarding such values as phantom. They are just what would have had to be set aside if the later plan had existed earlier. Such values can be omitted. This is the method used throughout the pension calculations in the present study.

To illustrate in more detail the actual calculation of the income values of pension benefits, we may use as a typical case that of an International Harvester officer, who joined the firm in 1928 and would normally retire at age sixty-five in 1971 after roughly 43 years of service. The career salary curve for the officer for the period 1928 to 1971 was constructed in the usual way in order to be able to obtain the values of his contributions, the benefits to him, the company-paid-for portion of the pension, the taxable pension, and the equivalent key.

Contributions were determined, using 5 per cent against salary for the earliest years of contribution, then 3 per cent of $3,000 and 6 per cent on the excess for the years through 1955, and 2 per cent of the excess over the base ($4,200, later $4,800) for later years. The amount at the year of retirement of all contributions, assuming interest accumulating at 4 per cent was also figured. As a practical matter, both figures were found simultaneously, using a standard prepared strip having on it amounts of one dollar at 4 per cent, and employing cumulative multiplication. In this case total contributions were $86,000, and contributions at interest amounted to $132,000.

The future service benefit was obtained by dividing total con-

58

tributions by three. This worked out to $29,000. To get the past service benefit, the salary total for the ten highest years was taken from the salary curve multiplied by 1.25 per cent and then by 11 years of service to get a past service benefit of about $11,000. The two parts together showed a total pension of slightly less than $40,000.[9] Checking this against the company's retirement policy of "making up the difference," the computed pension was found to exceed the minimum under the plan, so no further benefit was called for.[10]

The company-paid-for pension was determined by subtracting from the pension the annuity which the contributions at interest at the end of the year of retirement would buy. From tables we find that the annuity which one dollar will buy at 4 per cent for 15 years (normal expectation of life at retirement age sixty-five) is $.0899.[11] This was multiplied by the amount of the contributions at 4 per cent, which we found was $132,000, to get $12,-000. Subtracted from $40,000, this made the company-paid-for portion of the pension about $28,000.[12]

The taxable pension, however, is different. To find it, the technique used is essentially that provided for in the Internal Revenue Code of 1954. The idea is to learn how much the executive invested in the contract (excluding interest, which the government taxes), compare that with the value of the contract, and exclude from taxation that portion of the pension represented by his investment. The value of the contract in this instance was $40,000 (the pension) times 15 years, the expectation of life at age sixty-five, or $600,000. The investment in the contract

9. For pension calculations, survivorship options and other forms of alternative payment are not taken into account. Instead, all pensions are assumed to be paid in full as pensions, except for actuarial reductions for early retirement.

10. For most firms, the total pension was checked against estimated pensions shown in proxy statements. International Harvester showed only the company-paid-for portion of the pension, and this was checked as explained later. Some discrepancy due to different assumptions as to interest rates and other causes is to be expected.

11. Bogen, *op. cit.,* p. 1198, or Moore, *op. cit.,* p. 1126.

12. The proxy statement shows $20,000, but this executive will not retire until 1971, when his salary will doubtless be higher.

was $86,000 (the amount of the contributions). This was about 14 per cent of the value of the contract. The complement of this, 86 per cent, times the $40,000 pension left about $34,000 as the taxable pension. Then the taxable pension was spread over the 15 years of expected life after retirement.[13] For the executive, there was no other retirement income, so the taxable pension was the same as the adjusted gross income. To this, deductions and taxes were applied in the usual manner. Then, in the same way as for deferred cash under contract, the company-paid-for pension values at the year of retirement were computed—$309,000 before, $219,000 after taxes.

The equivalent key was then calculated, based on the years of service. In the same way as for deferred cash, fractions were derived and applied against salary to obtain income values. For 1958 the values were $7.8 thousand before and $5.5 thousand after taxes.

Most special measurement problems with pension plans arose in connection with early retirement or death of the executive. If an executive died, the benefit was, of course, not received, and so postretirement benefits—mostly pensions—were not reflected in company totals. For certain instances of death shortly after retirement the two-year rule (see note 13 below) was used. And for executives who retired before normal retirement age, the company's plan was examined to determine the executive's eligibility for a pension. Where a plan provided actuarial reduction factors, they were used. Where no factor was indicated, an

13. The pay-out period used for all multiple payment postretirement benefits was the expectation of life at the age of retirement, unless actual age at death was known. In such cases the actual period of retirement was used. For future retirement, normal retirement age sixty-five is assumed except in earlier years, when some companies specified a different age (age sixty for Shell Oil is a case in point). Where an executive died less than two years after retirement, no post-retirement benefits were figured. If he lived two years or more, benefits were computed. This is referred to as the two-year rule. Expectational figures were used for obtaining company-paid-for portions of pensions and for determining taxability of pensions. All data for life expectancy were taken from *Life Insurance Fact Book* (New York: Institute of Life Insurance, 1959), p. 111, Annuity Table for 1949—Male.

approximate factor was used, obtained by multiplying the number of years less than sixty-five at retirement times 6 per cent. This yielded the percentage reduction of the indicated pension. In a few instances where the plan specifically indicated no reduction for early retirement this was of course recognized. On all contributory plans in cases of late retirement, it has been assumed that both the employee's and the company's contributions were frozen at normal retirement age.

Income Values of Thrift Benefits

Another type of postretirement income is thrift plan benefits. The problem of measuring the income value to the executive of such benefits is fundamentally different from the problem of measuring other postretirement benefits. We do not need to worry about awards for future years or for missing past award years, or even about the shape of the salary curve for unknown years. This is so because thrift plan benefits, unlike other postretirement income, are taxed at capital gains rates; or, to put it another way, there is no need for finding the total benefit, since awards for all years will be taxed, not only at the same rate, but at a capital gains rate—25 per cent, except for executives retiring in 1952 and 1953, when the ratio was 26 per cent.

The only complexity in measuring thrift plan benefits arises in connection with income value after taxes, since the value before taxes is simply the amount set aside by the company for that year. The method which we have used is to obtain the present value of the tax, which will not be imposed until the year of retirement, and then to subtract it from the amount of the company set-aside. This gives us the present income value of the benefit.

Shell Oil Company was the first of the 25 largest manufacturing companies to have such a plan as reported in SEC records. The Shell Oil Company's provident fund—Het Voorzienings-

fonds der Verbonden Petroleum Maatschappyen[14]—was started
in the Netherlands in 1912 and introduced to Shell's United
States companies in 1917.[15] From the evidence it appears that the
fund provided originally for the employee's contributing up to
10 per cent of his pay with the company matching this dollar for
dollar, plus a profit contribution in good years. But there was a
roof on the employee's contributions of $480 per year, apparently
raised to about $1,000 by 1936, and removed altogether by 1942.

Specific provisions concerning the pay-out under the plan before 1944 make it appear[16] that the company contribution actually may have averaged around 10 per cent of the employee's pay,
despite the ceiling on what the employee paid in. These provisions
specified that the first installment, to be paid six months after
retirement, was to consist of $10,000 or the total of the em-
ployee's own contributions, whichever was greater. They also
specified that if the balance (the company's contributions and
presumably interest on the money) was more than $50,000, it
would be distributed in five annual installments starting one year
after the initial payment, with no installment under $10,000.

This original multiple-type payment was replaced by a lump
sum pay-out in 1944. When the company's pension plan was
installed, an offset was provided to reflect company payments
into the provident fund. Thus, in effect a life annuity plus a single
payment benefit were substituted for the previous payment in six
installments.

These earlier plan payments were handled in the same way as
deferred cash payments under contract (although included in
the thrift plan totals). All benefits paying out in 1944 and later
were treated according to the more typical capital gains concept.

An illustration is provided by a Shell executive's benefit for
1958. The executive's salary was $200,000. The company paid
into the fund 10 per cent of this or $20,000. But the executive

14. Annual Report to SEC, Form 10-K, 1936, Exhibit.
15. Kendall Beaton, *Enterprise in Oil* (New York: Appleton-Century-Crofts,
Inc., 1957), pp. 490–492.
16. Annual Report to SEC, Form 10-K, 1937, Exhibit A.

also contributed 10 per cent, so a total of $40,000 will accumulate interest at 4 per cent over seven years—1965, the year of expected retirement, minus 1958. These funds at interest will amount to $53,000. The capital gains tax of 25 per cent was applied to $53,000 less the $20,000 contributed by the officer, or about $33,000. The tax was thus a little over $8,000. The original amount contributed by the company ($20,000) was the before-tax income value. Subtracting from this the present value of the tax over seven years, which was around $6,000, gave an after-tax income value of a little less than $14,000.

Trends in Postretirement Benefits, 1929–1958

Having looked at the various problems inherent in the measurement of income values both before and after taxes for the various postretirement benefits, we may now turn our attention to trends in the 25-company totals—both as to rates of growth for different postretirement benefits, and as to what has happened to the make-up of the postretirement segment of the pay package.

Interpretation of the trends revealed in the diagrams which follow needs to be tempered by an understanding of the limitations of the data. Such limitations are more important here than was the case in the previous chapter relating to bonus trends. In general, this is true because of the greater extent of deferment. Other factors, however, also enter the picture.

Postretirement benefits, other than thrift plan gains which are not affected, are, in the calculation of income values, highly dependent on the shape of the career salary curve, of which parts are known with a high degree of certainty, while other parts are estimated. The nature of these estimates should be kept in mind, particularly as affecting the pension data. It must be stressed, however, that without such estimates there would be no income values.

Pension data are subject to other limitations as well. One of them concerns individual executives for whom no information could be obtained as to the facts relating to year of birth, year of joining company, year retired, or year of death. Such lack of information would have a definite effect on the calculation of income values. In the present study this information, where available, was tabulated for every executive. Where such figures were unavailable, estimates were made.

Another limitation concerns inadequacy of information on pension plans of some companies, or possible misinterpretation of the method of applying a company plan to a particular officer. First, in all cases where proxy data were readily available, they were used as a check on pension calculations. Such data, however, were not always available. Although lack of available information about, or possible misinterpretation of, plans caused difficulty in a few cases, a special pension plan worksheet was set up for every company in the study. Information on such plans was gathered from several sources and was in no way confined to spot years. It included much detail.

In the original computations for the present study, the possibility of a serious bias in the 25-company pension total was uncovered in scanning the behavior of the data for individual executives. In the early years, there were more blanks than for recent years for the income values of pensions. Some companies lacked plans in the early years. This was to be expected. But there is another factor. More of the 1929 executives had died or left the company before normal retirement age than is the case, say, for executives included among the top three in 1958, if for no other reason than merely because of the passage of time. Taking the two factors together, there was an overstatement of values for more recent years, and by contrast an understatement for the early years. This possible bias affected not only pension totals but the total pay package data as well.

The potential bias had to be corrected. The 25-company pension totals were divided by the number of executives included, to obtain an average income value per executive. Then the number of executives who died or left the company early, but who otherwise would have received pensions, was determined. The total number actually receiving benefits were added. The resulting totals were multiplied by the average income values to get a technically corrected set of 25-company pension amounts. These were obtained for each of the three highest paid executives for each spot year, both before and after taxes.[17] The new technically corrected pension figures used here differ little from the original figures in recent years, but are higher for the earlier years.

In a sense, a new bias has been introduced in that the pension totals for the entire 1929–1958 period are overstated, since some of the executives did, in fact, die, and since in the future some more of them will die. But the new figures can be justified as being roughly analogous to expectational data. This is true for the more recent years, and for many individual executives for whom no information on death was found in collecting personal data.

In theory, all postretirement benefits should be readjusted in the same way. As a practical matter, deferred benefits other than pensions are so little affected as not to merit reworking the data.

With these limitations in mind, rates of growth both before and after taxes of the chief elements of the postretirement pay package are brought out in Diagrams 8 and 9, which employ for this purpose the usual semilogarithmic grid. The diagrams bring out a few of the salient features.

The two diagrams differ little in the shape of the curves, which suggests that rates of growth were not greatly altered by the impact of taxes. But comparing levels of the data in the two diagrams does reveal a tax effect.

Pension values after taxes have had a long steady rise since 1937, and even then they were not far different from what they had been in 1929. Among the other benefits, thrift plan payments had by far the most rapid rate of growth, reaching in 1958 a level of about 20 times as high as in 1929. The net movement of stock and cash bonuses paid after retirement (here looked at in a new context) seems more hesitant than other indicators, but

17. Data on differentials in Chapter VIII and all other 25-company totals cited in this study reflect the technically corrected pension data.

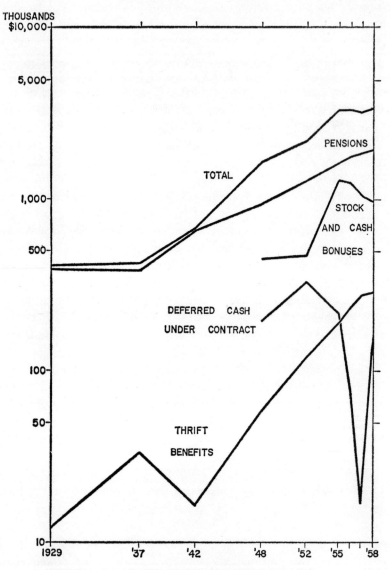

THOUSANDS
$10,000

5,000

PENSIONS

TOTAL

1,000

STOCK
AND CASH

500

BONUSES

DEFERRED CASH
UNDER CONTRACT

100

50

THRIFT
BENEFITS

10

1929   '37   '42   '48   '52   '55   '58

**Diagram 8—Postretirement Trends Before Taxes,
Top Three Together**

66

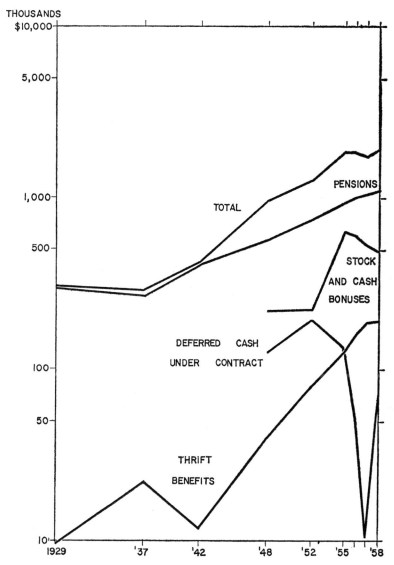

THOUSANDS

$10,000

5,000

PENSIONS

1,000

TOTAL

500

STOCK
AND CASH
BONUSES

DEFERRED   CASH

UNDER   CONTRACT

100

50

THRIFT

BENEFITS

10

1929   '37   '42   '48   '52   '55   '58

Diagram 9—Postretirement Trends After Taxes, Top Three Together

67

there is little doubt of the general upward thrust. The erratic movement of the line for deferred cash under contract, highlighted by the drastic dip in 1957, cannot safely be summarized for trend, since only a handful of executives are included.[18]

If the total of all postretirement income values is taken as 100 per cent, we can look at the different shares which each benefit represents of the total. This is done in Diagrams 10 and 11. Since the two diagrams show little difference between the before- and after-tax views, only the after-tax picture need be discussed.

Pensions, though down from almost 100 per cent of the total, still accounted in 1958 for close to 60 per cent of the postretirement pay package of top executives. Thrift plans rose from 3 per cent of the total but were still only 10 per cent as of 1958. Deferred cash payments under contract which did not even show in 1942, have fluctuated, but in 1958 they stood at 4 per cent of the whole. Deferred cash and stock bonuses, also a recent development, accounted for more than one-fourth of the postretirement total in 1958.

The Retirement Age of Top Executives

A further question that arises in connection with retirement benefits is whether a trend toward earlier retirement has developed, which could mean changes in personnel policy with regard to retirement. The present study for the period 1929–1958 does not support the contention that there is such a trend.

In order to test the hypothesis, the 178 executives included in the present study, for whom definite information was available as to age at retirement, were tabulated as to age and year of retirement. Now if there were a trend to earlier retirement, we should expect to find fewer executives retiring after age sixty-five and more retiring before age sixty-five. The tabulation was grouped

18. A sample of firms larger than the 25-company sample used in the present study would presumably yield more reliable evidence of trend.

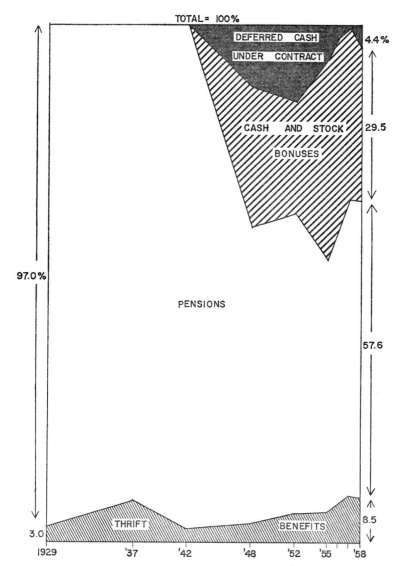

TOTAL = 100%

DEFERRED CASH UNDER CONTRACT — 4.4%

CASH AND STOCK BONUSES — 29.5

PENSIONS — 57.6

97.0%

THRIFT BENEFITS — 8.5

3.0

1929   '37   '42   '48   '52   '55   '58

**Diagram 10—Postretirement Package Before Taxes,
Top Three Together**

69

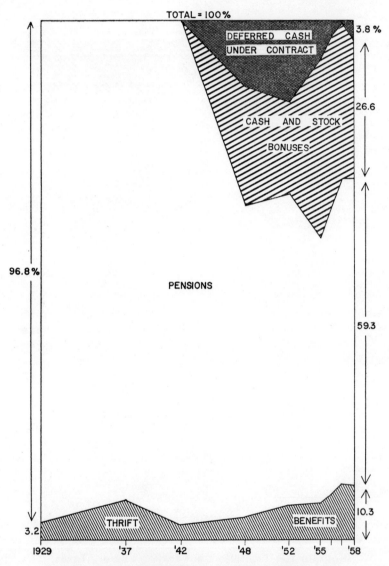

TOTAL = 100%

3.8 %

DEFERRED CASH
UNDER CONTRACT

26.6

CASH AND STOCK

BONUSES

96.8%

PENSIONS

59.3

10.3

THRIFT

BENEFITS

3.2

1929   '37   '42   '48   '52   '55   '58

**Diagram 11—Postretirement Package After Taxes,
Top Three Together**

70

into two periods—1929–1943 and 1944–1958. It was also broken down as to age at retirement into two parts: before sixty-five and sixty-five and over.

Table 8—Age and Year of Retirement for 178 Corporate Executives

Age at Retirement	YEAR RETIRED 1929–1943	1944–1958	Total
Under 51	3	1	4
51–55	5	2	7
56–60	10	10	20
61–65	17	48	65
66–70	19	36	55
71–75	6	10	16
76–80	2	7	9
Over 80	—	2	2
All Ages	62	116	178

Using the more condensed version of Table 8, a chi-square test was applied. This revealed that the observed difference in retirement ages between the two time periods had no statistical significance; it could easily have occurred by chance.[19] This confirms Roberts' conclusion that:

The opinions of business men and researchers are mixed, but few hold that the use of deferred compensation has had much effect on retirement age. The consensus appears to be that it has lowered the average retirement age slightly if at all.[20]

19. While a 5 per cent level of significance is often used in a case of this kind, the resulting chi-square fell in the neighborhood of the 50 per cent level of significance.
20. David R. Roberts, *Executive Compensation* (Glencoe: The Free Press of Glencoe, 1959), p. 146.

IV

Stock Option and Purchase Gains

Stock option and purchase gains, whose importance has been heightened by the special tax treatment accorded them recently, provide an element of flexibility in the top executive pay package that does not exist with other pay items. If an executive is granted an option, the choice of when he will receive income benefits is not, as for most other pay items, solely in the company's power. The officer can at least in some degree take his income when he wants it. Option gains, of course, constitute what is in a way a borderline type of income—going to an executive partly in his capacity as an executive, but also involving his role as an investor. In this study we shall regard them as the former.

Because of their capital gains aspect, such gains present special problems in the determination of income values. Here we shall explore the income values for this type of gain, and analyze option trends for the 25-company sample.

Stock Option Gains

A stock option in its simplest form is the right given to an employee to buy his company's stock at close to today's price sometime in the future. The effectiveness of the option as a compensation device rests on the expectation that the price of the company's stock will rise. If the price rises in due course, the executive may then exercise his option or right to buy the stock. An immediate gain results from the excess of the new price of the stock over the original or option price. Of course, the employee can hold on to the stock, and if the price continues to rise he will have a further gain if he sells it. If on the contrary, there is no rise at all in the price of the stock and the price actually falls, the employee does not have to exercise his option, and therefore need suffer no loss.

Stock option gains are now given special tax treatment. Before 1950, such gains were generally considered fully taxable. Since then, however, by the Revenue Act of 1950, new provisions, later included as Section 421 of the Internal Revenue Code of 1954, have come into effect. Under the new legislation, provided certain conditions are met, stock option gains become taxable only after the stock purchased under option is sold, and then only at long-term capital gains rates (25 per cent, except during the war in Korea when the rate was 26 per cent). Such benefits were given to option plans which qualified as "restricted stock option plans." Some of the more important restrictions,[1] insofar as they affect any of the 25 largest manufacturing companies, are that the option price must be not less than 95 per cent of the fair market value per share on the date when the option is granted; that stock purchased under option cannot be sold sooner than two years after the date of the grant; and that stock purchased under option must be held at least six months before

1. These provisions are spelled out in more detail in the various tax service publications, for example: Commerce Clearing House, *Federal Tax Course 1958*, pp. 2011–2015.

74

it is sold. Moreover, the option is nontransferable except after death, and in the event of death the option must be exercised by the employee's executor within one year after the employee's death. If the individual ceases to be employed by the company, he must exercise his option within three months after the end of his employment, while options granted on or after June 22, 1954, must be exercised within ten years.

As we have already pointed out, the gain from a stock option can be divided into two parts. First, there is the difference between the market price and the option price at the time of exercise. Second, there is also the difference between the market price at the time of exercise and at the time of later sale, assuming there is a sale.[2]

As to the first part of the gain, there is little doubt that it accrues to the executive primarily in his role as a corporate executive, not as an investor. This part of the gain is therefore treated as part of the pay package. By contrast, the second part of the gain, representing the rise in price from the time of exercise to the time of sale, is received by an executive primarily in his role as an investor. This part of the gain is therefore excluded from the top executive pay package.

Implicit in the conclusion to limit consideration to the first of the two segments of the potential capital gain, is the assumption that this portion of the gain will not be reduced or eliminated by a loss during the later period. Whether this will happen depends on such factors as the course of the market, the strategy pursued by the executive, and the keenness of his sense of timing.

If the executive's strategy is to maximize the spread between option price and market price, and if this strategy is reasonably successful, the executive will have bought close to the top of the market, which means that the risk of a fall during the six months'

2. The executive can, of course, hold the stock and never sell it, accumulating dividends as an investor. Then there is no realized capital gain and the executive is taxed only on the dividends. These, however, are fully taxable except for the dividend credit, and this credit must compete with the even more favorable tax provisions for capital gains under restricted stock option plans.

minimum holding period necessary to get capital gains tax treatment on sale of the stock will be greatly increased.

One possible course of action for the executive at this time is to insure himself against a loss. As has been pointed out in an AFL-CIO publication, in substantially the following terms, the executive can

protect himself against the drop in the value of the stock even after he purchases it by entering into an agreement called a "put" giving him the option to sell the shares at the then current market price. Eventually, if he decided to exercise this option to sell he could still pocket the difference between the option price and market price (except for the cost of the "put") regardless of how low the shares had dropped in the interim.[3]

Another course of action would be for the executive to bide his time for a couple of years, and take a chance on a future recovery in the price of the stock before selling. This way he could keep all of the gain, at least before taxes. For those companies among the 25 largest manufacturers having stock option plans, this would seem to be the better of the two strategies, in the absence of storm warnings indicating a major depression.[4]

In either case it is unlikely that later sale of the stock will wipe out completely the first part of the capital gain—that which takes place at the time of exercise of the option. What typically happens to stock purchased under option is unclear due to inadequate reporting under SEC Regulations, but a trial run using five executives (all of whom were at one time in the top three) in one of the 25 largest manufacturing companies for the period 1954 through July 1958, revealed the following:

	Shares Bought Under Option	Shares Sold
Mr. A	18,000	7,200
Mr. B	9,900	3,400
Mr. C	16,906	0
Mr. D	13,000	0
Mr. E	9,675	1,925[5]

3. Industrial Union Department, AFL–CIO, *The Stock Option Scandal,* p. 5.

4. Under certain conditions, especially for an executive close to retirement, the use of the "put" would appear to be almost a must if the executive wished to protect his gain.

5. Executive died during period.

7 6

To measure the income value of stock option gains, two approaches are possible. One is to use the present value approach, the other is to measure the current income. A variation of the current income approach would be to assume that the gain per share at the time of exercise should apply to all shares granted regardless of whether they were exercised. This, like the present value approach, takes care of unexercised shares. Aside from the lack of realism, a problem arises as to how to distribute the unexercised shares over the years. Shares are not in fact all exercised at the same time. An executive may exercise options under two or more grants in a single year, or may buy up the stock under one year's award in erratic fashion over a number of years. For these reasons, the current income approach used in the present study recognizes only actual exercise of options and disregards unexercised shares.

If we regard stock option gains as being similar to deferred bonuses in stock, for example, we can apply a present value approach. To illustrate: if it were known what typically happened to optioned stock in the 25 largest companies, we could estimate the average period of time elapsing between grant of an option and its exercise. For the sake of argument, say this worked out to five years. Then stock prices of each of the companies having option plans could be forecast, using some average yearly rate of advance such as 5 per cent over the five years. The amount of the gain could be determined by getting the difference between the forecast market price and the known option price, and multiplying by the number of shares. Finally, after allowing for the capital gains tax, we could, using the present value of one dollar at 4 per cent for five years, determine the value of the gain at the time of grant both before and after taxes. An underlying assumption of this method is that the option is exercised for all shares. While the method avoids the difficulty of accounting for unexercised shares, it involves hazardous estimates as to timing of the exercise of options and forecasts of stock prices.

In contrast to the present value approach, a current income approach can be built on a more solid foundation. Proxy statements for those firms among the 25 largest manufacturing companies having stock option plans typically report pertinent details of options exercised by any of the three highest paid officers. Details reported include shares, option prices, and market prices at the time of exercise. These facts usually reflect any stock splits and dividends in stock.[6]

By taking the number of shares for which options are exercised and multiplying it by the difference between the option price and market price at the time of exercise, we can arrive at the amount of the unrealized capital gain. This produces an income value on a current income basis. The 25 per cent long-term capital gains tax can be applied directly to this amount to get the after-tax benefit. While this method excludes any possible benefit from unexercised stock options, it is realistic. It reveals more surely what has actually happened. It relies more on factual evidence and less on forecasts of prices and timing. But even though we use a current income approach for the present study, we still can continue to regard stock option gains as a form of deferred payment.

The exercise of an option by a Republic Steel executive in 1957 provides a good illustration of how the income value of a stock option gain, both before and after taxes, was determined. This officer exercised an option to buy 13,000 shares at $20.56 per share when the market price was $58.00. The $58.00 less $20.56 gave him a margin of $37.44 per share. This, times the 13,000 shares, produced an unrealized capital gain upon exercise of roughly $487,000, the before-tax income value of the stock option gain. Since the applicable long-term capital gains rate was 25 per cent, the complement, 75 per cent,[7] was multiplied by the before-tax value to get an after-tax income value for the option gain of $365,000.

6. A technical problem, that of the overlap in the reporting of options exercised, made it necessary to check proxy statements for any given year with those for adjacent years and also against SEC Form 4's to avoid duplication.

7. This rate was used for all years except 1952 and 1953, when 26 per cent was used.

Stock Purchase Gains

Stock purchase gains as treated in this chapter are uniquely represented in Union Carbide's stock purchase plan. This plan, as it operated from 1946 to 1958, should be distinguished from other stock purchase plans. It did not involve the individual contributions and matching company amounts characterizing savings and thrift plans. Nor did it entail the sale of stock currently at a bargain price, typical of many stock purchase plans. Instead, stock was offered from time to time at 100 per cent of market (although the plan required sale only at not less than 75 per cent of market) to company employees, generally including the top officers.

Each executive who received an offering of stock paid for it, not with cash, but by becoming indebted to his company. The stock was to serve as collateral until the debt was paid. Nonetheless, the offering was considered a "purchase" by the executive and was so reported to SEC on his Form 4.[8] Since the shares were sold at market, some people have assumed that no income accrued to the executive. It was thought to be analogous to buying an automobile on time.

In the search for economic realities as distinct from legal form, one can understand better what had been happening by posing a few questions about the plan: (1) When did the shares of stock come into the physical possession of the executive? (2) What did the executive do with his money? (3) When did the capital gain take place?

Under the plan shares were to be delivered not at the time of offer or "purchase" but later in blocks of 25 shares as they became fully paid for.[9] Under the option plan typical for companies among the 25 largest firms, the shares are delivered when paid

8. A form on which stockholdings and stock transactions of officers and directors are reported to SEC.
9. During the time the stock was not yet paid for, it was pledged as collateral against the debt.

for in full at the time the option is exercised. Thus the movement of shares is similar.

What actually happened to the executive's money is also revealing. The mode of payment pointed to in the proxy statements for the earlier years was that dividends on the stock not yet delivered or paid for were used to pay the interest at 2 per cent on the executive's outstanding indebtedness, and that any excess would be applied against the principal of the debt, thus freeing shares of stock. Under the original plan, shares in each offering would have to be paid for within five years, although the board of directors could extend this period. It was clearly implied that in addition to allowing dividends in excess of interest to pay off the debt, an executive might have to make additional payments. The latter, however, was not stressed.

The financial records submitted to the SEC nevertheless indicated that a shift of emphasis took place—away from the painless self-financing approach. The records show that from 1949 on, the deliveries of shares to executives under the plan resulted mostly from additional payments, and only to a lesser extent from the excess of dividends over interest.[10]

After Congress had approved the new "restricted stock option" legislation, payments were brought into closer conformity with the stock option principle. The board of directors provided in 1951 that henceforth only half of the dividends on the pledged stock had to be applied against interest on the debt or against the debt itself. At the same time, the board provided that shares under the first offering, which had occurred in 1946, would be extended as to time of payment of the outstanding indebtedness for another five years—a total period of ten years, corresponding to the maximum ten-year period allowed under the "restricted stock option" arrangement. Since 1951, other offerings have been extended in the same way.

Thus, the mechanism which made the Union Carbide plan work, particularly after 1950, was essentially the same as that for a stock option plan. The price at which the stock would be

10. Annual Report to SEC, Form 10-K, Schedule II.

bought was fixed in advance at a level likely to be exceeded. The bulk of the executive's money—in the form of additional payments—was kept out of action until after a substantial rise in the price of the stock. In other words, the objective was to maximize the gap between the offering price and the market price at the time of delivery.

In line with the earlier discussion of stock options, the gain on shares already in the physical possession of the executive (and fully paid for) became a layer of income going to him primarily in his capacity as an investor rather than as a corporate executive, since the gain in value from this point on might be achieved by any other investor (assuming he is affluent). But every share actually paid for and delivered, whether through the operation of the dividend-exceeds-interest provision or through the larger additional payments, gave the executive a capital gain to the extent of the difference between the offering price on the share and its market price at the time of delivery. Delivery, then, is the point at which the capital gain under the Union Carbide stock purchase plan has been recognized for this study.

While not necessarily typical, the example of one officer will serve to illustrate the nature and extent of the gains possible under the plan. The analysis will be confined to the officer's 1955 gains. He received offerings over several years as indicated below.[11] The data have been adjusted for the 1948 three-for-one

Date	Shares	Price Per Share
April 1946	6,000	$38.67
June 1947	6,000	33.46
April 1948	6,000	34.83
June 1953	10,000	62.25
July 1955	10,000	98.50

stock split. Also available and of value was the total number of shares still unpaid for and undelivered for the years from the beginning of 1951 to the beginning of 1959.[12] In addition, there were other data in connection with extending the time for pay-

11. *Ibid.*
12. *Ibid.*

81

ment, indicating that the undelivered portion of the 1947 award stood at 5,150 shares in June, 1952, and that the undelivered portion of the 1948 award was 5,225 shares in April, 1953, all shares reflecting the split.[13]

Using these elements of information, an inventory diagram was made showing graphically the outstanding shares in each year's award, the inventory strips adding up to the total unpaid for shares. Diagram 12 as shown here is only an approximation of a diagram which had lines so precise they had to be worked out using ship's curves. It does bring out the idea, however. From the diagram it was possible to estimate the deliveries during 1955 under each offering. For each delivery, the average of the high and low for 1955 was taken as the market price. The rest of the process was similar to the calculation of a stock option gain.

For the 1947 award the shares as estimated from the diagram as being delivered in 1955 were 4,750. The market price of $98.32 less the offering price of $33.46 left a margin of $64.86. The $64.86 times the 4,750 shares gave a capital gain of about $308,000. Capital gains from other years' awards, however, brought the total to $1,305,000 before taxes, the income value before taxes of the 1955 captal gains from the stock purchase plan. In 1955, the executive apparently also was paid directly the excess of dividends over interest on the debt to the extent of $10,000. This was included in fully taxable income. The total stock purchase benefit before taxes, including the dividend excess, was more than $1,315,000. After taxes (mostly at the 25 per cent long-term rate), the corresponding figure was roughly $984,000.

Stock Option and Purchase Gains, 1929–1958

Having considered the measurement of the unrealized capital gains, both before and after taxes, arising out of the stock option

13. Proxy statements.

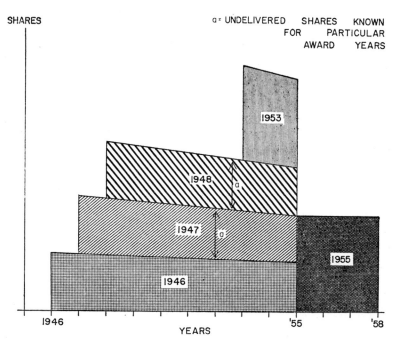

SHARES

a = UNDELIVERED SHARES KNOWN FOR PARTICULAR AWARD YEARS

1953

1948

a

1947

a

1946

1955

1946   YEARS   '55   '58

Diagram 12—Inventory of Shares (Schematic)

8 3

and purchase plans, we may turn now to what the 25-company totals demonstrate. The data on the totals are set forth in Diagrams 13 and 14. There are certain limitations of the data which should be kept in mind, however. They bear on the incompleteness of earlier records, the extent to which gains actually will be realized, and the difference between the granting and the exercise of options.

For example, the option gains shown for 1929 may be understated. Company records, including annual reports, bear evidence of many stock purchase and bonus plans offering shares to executives at bargain prices, often through indirect schemes such as management trusts. The extent of such benefits was probably underreported in the 1929 FTC data. On the other hand, gains from such plans were often illusory, since they were wiped out by the stock price declines of the 1930s.

Stock option and purchase gains shown in both diagrams are the amounts of unrealized capital gains resulting from the exercise of options. Whether or not such gains actually have been or will be realized depends on the prices at which stock purchased under option is later sold. Where such prices fall below the option price, except in cases in which a "put" affords protection, the gain will be less. On the other hand, to the extent prices rise, the total gain will be greater. As indicated earlier, however, the portion of the gain from the time of exercise of the option to the time of sale is regarded as being primarily of an investment nature and therefore is not included.

Finally, option gains are recorded at the time of exercise of the option. This gives prompt recognition of the unrealized capital gain when it occurs, but can mislead the unwary as to the trend. Option grants have tended to rise along with salary. Thus even if exercise of options was limited in 1958, this does not of itself point to a bleak future for option gains.

Two contrasting items of the pay package—salary and stock option and purchase gains—are pictured in Diagram 13. The data are 25-company totals for the three highest paid officers taken together. The diagram shows that gains, while of course

84

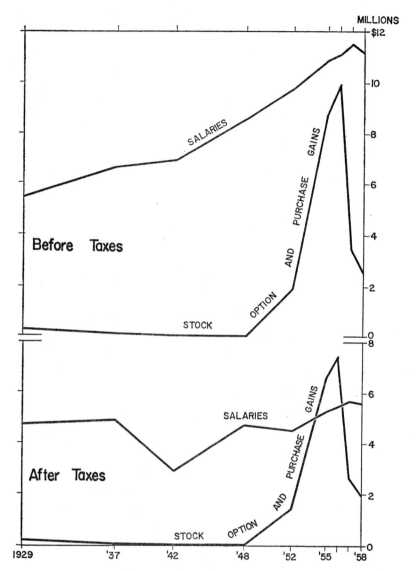

MILLIONS

$12

10

8

6

4

2

0

SALARIES

PURCHASE GAINS

OPTION AND

Before Taxes

STOCK

8

6

4

2

0

SALARIES

PURCHASE GAINS

OPTION AND

After Taxes

STOCK

1929   '37   '42   '48   '52   '55   '58

Diagram 13—Salaries and Option Gains, Top Three Together

8 5

showing some loss through taxes, are much the same shape whether looked at before or after taxes. But the contrast in the impact of the federal income tax on the two pay items is strongly evidenced by the way the two curves behave against each other. Before taxes, the option gain curve, reaching upward like a giant stalagmite, never quite touches the salary curve; after taxes the option stalagmite cuts a big hole through the fallen salary roof, rising above it in both 1955 and 1956.

Stock option and purchase gains, of relatively little significance in the 1929–1948 period, ran into millions of dollars in the period 1952–1958. Before taxes they were only around two million dollars in 1952, but reached a peak of close to ten million in 1956. By 1958, however, they had dropped back close to two million again. Such behavior would seem to be evidence of an erratic and unstable element in the executive pay package, especially if compared with salary.

Stock option and purchase gains for the peak year, 1956, are shown by company in Diagram 14. The totals in the diagram include only those executives who actually exercised options in 1956. Many did not do so. As a result, some of the bars include only one executive, some two, and some all three. From an analysis of the diagram, it is evident that there was little concentration of option gains in any particular industry. While five oil companies appeared, non-oil companies predominated. One oil company was the highest, but three others were below the $500,000 mark. Of the two automobile companies, one was second from the top, but the other ranked last. Although one steel company was near the top of the list, the other was close to the bottom. Other industries—electrical, chemical, rubber, and nonferrous metals—were also represented by companies which reported stock option or purchase gains. The gains shown for Union Carbide are stock purchase gains. As a further illustration of the erratic nature of option and purchase gains, the same company's executives in 1955 showed gains before taxes of around $1,890,000.

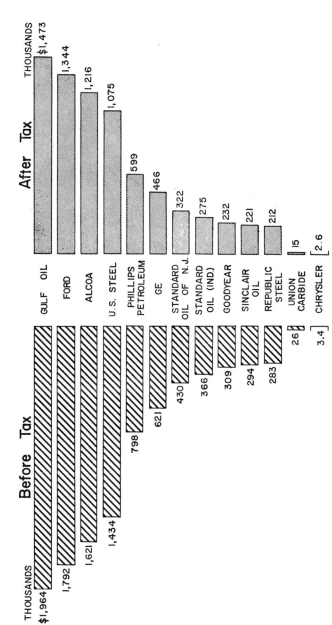

Diagram 14—Stock Option and Purchase Gains in 1956, Top Three Together

8 7

A Few Critical Questions

As one might well imagine from our discussion of income values and trends for stock option and purchase gains, many questions have arisen about this form of remuneration of executives. We defer consideration of two of the larger questions to later chapters, namely: are stock options discriminatory? And what effect do option gains have on pay differentials among the highest paid officers? Other questions, however, remain to be answered. What effect do options have on the stockholder? How do such devices as contingent credits and dividend units relate to options? And what effect, if any, do options have on the price of a company's stock, or on the firm's earnings?

Stock option plans come under fire from critics because of the unfavorable effects which the plans are believed to have on the position of the outside stockholder. Among other facts, critics often point both to the dilution of equity of the individual stockholder as a result of the issue of stock under options,[14] and the loss to stockholders and to the company resulting from the purchase by the company of its own stock on the market and later reissue of shares to executives at lower prices.[15]

On the first point, the extent of dilution depends mainly on how the stock is acquired. If the company buys up its own shares on the market, to be resold later to optionees, any outside shareholder who keeps his stock actually has an increase in his equity, since outstanding shares are temporarily reduced, while his own shares remain unchanged. Of course, when the shares are issued again, the reverse takes place. His equity in percentage terms is reduced, but only back to where it was in the first place.

If, instead of reacquired stock, authorized but unissued shares,

14. William A. Doyle, "Do Stock Options Dilute the Equity?" *N.Y. World-Telegram & Sun*, Feb. 16, 1960.

15. U.S. SEC, Division of Corporate Regulation, *Proposed Findings and Conclusions of the Division of Corporate Regulation in the Matter of Middle South Utilities, Inc.*, File No. 70–3777, p. 51. Also, Industrial Union Department, AFL–CIO, *op. cit.*, p. 25.

or newly issued shares, are employed, the equity of the outside shareholder is diluted. How serious the dilution is, depends on such factors as the proportion of newly issued shares, the total shares outstanding, and the life of the plan.

In this connection the example of Standard Oil of New Jersey is fairly typical. The company's most recent stock option plan provides for use not only of reacquired shares but also of authorized but unissued shares. The plan allows for a maximum of three million shares to be sold under options over a period of up to 15 years from the start of the plan. Under this plan, there is little likelihood that all shares will be distributed in any one year. The three million maximum proposed for the option route was less than 1.5 per cent of the 214,006,427 shares outstanding.[16] Dilution of the equity in this instance would not appear to be a serious matter.

With regard to the second point, where shares are sold under option at prices well below the market price at the time of exercise, the book value per share afterwards would be less than if the same shares were sold at market. This does not mean, however, that the company need suffer great loss in buying shares at market and reselling to executives at the option price. If most of the shares can be purchased at the time the options are granted, or at other times when stock prices are low, the gap between option and market price at the time of purchase by the company, and the consequent loss, can be minimized.

Although some people may find this surprising, it appears that in spite of dilution of equity, possible loss in book value of shares, or loss to the company in resale to executives of reacquired stock, the market for the stock is typically little affected.[17] In fact one financial columnist has stated, "The actual value of the shares may not be too greatly changed."[18] As another observer puts it, "The stock market with its usual heedlessness,

16. Proxy statement, April 10, 1959.
17. Referred to here is only the immediate effect of options, and not the longer run effects which are of a different character.
18. Doyle, *op. cit.*

applies the same basis of valuation to common shares whether warrants (options) are outstanding or not."[19]

Contingent credits and dividend units were referred to in Chapter II in the discussion of short-term deferred stock bonuses. These are the special compensation devices developed by GM and Du Pont to protect executives covered by option grants in the event of a decline in the price of the company's stock.

Under the GM bonus plan as modified in 1957, the bonus given to an executive who was granted an option was set at 75 per cent of the bonus he would otherwise have received, this amount to be wholly in cash. Along with the option, a contingent credit in the form of shares of stock was provided, in an amount equal at the time of the award to one-third of the bonus actually awarded. Taken together, the contingent credit and the bonus would total to the amount of bonus which the executive otherwise would have received. The number of shares under the option was set at three times the number of shares in the executive's contingent credit. As option shares were exercised, the contingent credit would be reduced in the same proportion. Any shares left over in the contingent credit, provided the option was not fully exercised, would be delivered upon the expiration of the option in five equal installments, presumably also including dividends accumulated on the stock. The options were to expire ten years after the date of grant.[20]

The Du Pont device included as its C Bonus Plan was reported first at about the same time as the GM arrangement. Under the Du Pont plan, one and one-half dividend units were awarded for each share of stock or cash equivalent, which otherwise would have been awarded under the usual Class B bonus. Shares of stock optioned to any person would not be more than one and one-third times the number of dividend units awarded. For every four shares of stock bought under options, three dividend units would be canceled.[21] Dividend units were to start at the date of

19. Benjamin Graham and David L. Dodd, *Security Analysis* (New York: McGraw-Hill, 1951), 3rd ed., p. 572.
20. Company Annual Report for 1957, pp. 27–28.
21. Proxy statement, special meeting of stockholders, October 7, 1957.

grant of the option.[22] And only the unused portions of the dividend units were to be canceled on exercise of all or part of an option.

The alternate pay arrangements provided by both of the above plans can be brought into sharper focus by a specific comparison in terms of the stock involved. Let us assume that at General Motors the bonus foregone is 1,000 shares of stock delivered in five equal yearly installments, at Du Pont, 1,000 shares in four equal yearly installments. At GM, 1,000 shares would be delivered in five equal yearly installments after the option expired if it were not exercised, or 3,000 shares might be bought over a period of ten years if it were. At Du Pont, 1,500 dividend units would be given, with payment starting at the grant of the option, if it were not exercised, or 2,000 shares might be bought in eight years should the executive choose to exercise the option.

The generous nature of the alternatives compared to the amount of bonus which would otherwise be received is obvious—a generosity which has evoked from some observers a "You can't lose!" designation. If the price of the stock should fall instead of rise and the executive did not exercise his option, it is clear that in both companies he would be better off than if he instead received the added amount due him under the regular bonus plan. This is so for General Motors, because dividends would have accumulated for a much longer period of time with later distribution of the stock. In the Du Pont case, no stock would be received, but this is made up for by dividends on 500 additional shares. Moreover, the dividend units start paying off immediately, even if the option is to be exercised eventually. Thus the executive gets the benefit either way.[23]

On the other hand, if the second alternative comes into play and the option is exercised, the executive will still be materially

22. "A dividend unit entitles the recipient to receive until death or age 85 whichever is later cash equal to the dividends paid on one share of the company's stock." Annual report to SEC, Form 10-K, 1957.

23. It can even be argued that he receives it both ways, since when dividends on 1,500 shares stop on exercise of the option, dividends on 2,000 shares purchased under option start, and continue at least until the stock is sold, always assuming there is a sale.

better off than with the amount he would otherwise receive as a regular bonus, first, because of the eight- to ten-year period during which the market price is on the average, likely to rise, and second, because any thinness of margin between market and option price is made up for by the fact that the shares under option are a multiple of the number of shares of regular bonus foregone.

Our third question, about the effect of stock options on the price of common stocks, has come recently into hot dispute as a result of the findings of the Division of Corporate Regulation of the Securities and Exchange Commission in the Middle South Utilities case. This report concluded:

With respect to the frequently asserted contention that stock options are, in effect, a prime mover (upwards of course) of market prices of common stocks, we submit that circumstances other than stock options are determinative of market price movements. The increase in the market prices of common stocks over, say, the past decade, is attributable, in large measure, to general market, economic and monetary conditions rather than to any effort of management.[24]

It must be said, however, that when one is dealing with the 25 largest manufacturing companies, the external conditions cited above are not as independent as is commonly thought. The reason is that the policy-making decisions of management in the larger companies have at least some influence on these conditions.

It is possible, as suggested by SEC's Division of Corporate Regulation and by others, that changes in stock prices for companies which have options outstanding are determined largely by market forces and related factors. However, it would be naïve to contend that the performance of executives had no influence on the outcome. As pointed out earlier, the objective is to maximize the gap; and the executives of larger companies are uniquely situated to play, not only upon external factors, but upon internal ones as well.

For example, the president and chairman of the board of a smaller company, particularly well qualified to judge such matters, has stated cynically of stock option and similar plans that

24. Division of Corporate Regulation, SEC, *op. cit.*, p. 34.

they were devices "dreamed up by clever men to soak up the gravy." He cited the inner workings of the stock purchase plan of one of the larger companies in which he was formerly a vice-president. The company in question had a plan which allowed officers to pay for the stock over a period of time, even though sales were recognized at the time of offering. He described the inner strategy of the plan about as follows:

The company kept inventories and profits low, and all sorts of pressure was put on the balance sheet and the profit and loss account to keep the market price of the stock low before the offering price was set.

A little later on, the management, taking maximum advantage of its internal knowledge, did everything to swell inventories, build assets, and favor the balance sheet and profit and loss statement. Then they called in the financial analysts to point out the beautiful and of course improved future prospects. These were talked up, executives radiated confidence, and stock prices rose.

When prices had risen to a certain point, it was felt that this sort of thing might be overdone if it was carried too far. Then some of the executives paid up their indebtedness, took delivery on the stock, and sold it, racking up fat capital gains.

More recently the company turned about and tightened the balance sheet, sought to make earnings look thin, etc. And so the cycle starts over again.[25]

Thus it appears that, at least for the largest companies, the price of the firm's stock is influenced greatly by external factors, to some degree by internal manipulation, and probably to a lesser extent by the officer's performance on the job. Aside from the tax advantage, it would therefore seem that stock options are far from an ideal method of compensation in the sense of relating reward to effort.

The question of whether stock options tend to boost corporate earnings more than would otherwise be the case has also been probed by SEC's Division of Corporate Regulation. The division took the earnings per share both for the year before a stock option plan went into effect in 12 electric utility companies, and for

25. Confidential interview. The plan cited here was for a company not included in the 25 largest. The plan, however, appears to be similar to the original Union Carbide plan described earlier.

the year ending in mid-1959, in order to measure the supposed effect of stock option plans in terms of the percentage increase in the earnings per share. The performance of the 12 electric utility companies having stock option plans was compared with that of 12 registered electric holding company systems that did not have such plans.

The Division found that the earnings per share for the non-option companies showed a greater percentage rise than those for the stock option companies. The report concluded:

In the light of the superior earnings performance of the non-stock option companies as contrasted with the stock option companies there is serious question, at least as to public utility companies, whether the existence of stock options can be said to play a significant part in a company's earnings performance.[26]

The later Findings and Opinion of the SEC rejected the findings of its Division of Corporate Regulation in the Middle South Utilities case. The Commission said in part:

We do not consider that any valid conclusions can be drawn from these figures. Not only is the sampling very small but it is clearly quite impossible to isolate and compensate for the many irrelevant factors affecting the operations of the various companies selected for the comparison.[27]

The truth may lie somewhere between the two quotations. Although many complicating factors influence the nicety of the comparisons, even the limited evidence raises a serious doubt about the favorable effect of options on increased earnings, at least for the utility companies sampled. The effect in manufacturing companies, as distinct from electric utilities, of stock options on earnings per share should be an interesting subject for further investigation in the light of the above findings.

26. U.S. SEC, Division of Corporate Regulation, *op. cit.*, p. 34.
27. U.S. SEC, *Findings and Opinion of the Commission in the Matter of Middle South Utilities, Inc.,* File No. 70–3777, p. 5.

V

Pay Elements
Not Included
in the Package

.

There are certain items in an executive's pay which are not usually included in the study of the total package, because the extent of the benefits received cannot be accurately determined. We, too, shall omit them from the total pay package, which, in this study does include the major elements, but we shall discuss these items, and where the data warrant it, consider the extent of the benefits received.

The missing pay elements fall into two classes. The first includes items, such as life insurance premiums, certain gains from security transactions, and benefits from management trusts, which are difficult to measure or where company reporting is incomplete or inconsistent. The second category comprises items for which there is no numerical evidence in the records of the Federal Trade Commission or the Securities and Exchange Commission. All of these are tied in with executive expense accounts.

Elements Which are Partially Reported or Hard to Measure

Life insurance benefits are a good example of a pay item omitted for lack of complete or consistent reporting. Although 11 out of the 39 companies in the present study reported officers receiving insurance benefits paid for in whole or in part by the company, the reporting of this item was marginal through 1952 and almost nonexistent thereafter. In 1952, only 6 out of 25 companies reported such benefits, and only one firm has done so in any year since 1952.

The reason for the incomplete reporting of benefits is tied in with requirements of the SEC. The instructions of November 2, 1949, which were still in effect in 1952, called for the reporting as to each of the three highest paid executives of

money paid, set aside or accrued pursuant to any pension, retirement, savings or other similar plan including premiums paid for life insurance or retirement annuities. However, premiums paid for group life insurance need not be included if it is impractical to do so and if there is set forth in a note the amount of such insurance purchased for each individual officer or director.[1]

Then according to the instructions as revised for 1954 and later, the requirement was further weakened:

Information need not be included as to payments to be made for, or benefits to be received from, group life or accident insurance, group hospitalization or similar group payments or benefits.[2]

On the basis of these regulations, most firms providing life insurance protection reported only the combined payments for a group life insurance and pension plan. Four companies, however, showed life insurance payments separately, as follows:

1. U.S. SEC, Instructions for preparing Form 10-K, revised Nov. 2, 1949.
2. U.S. SEC, Instructions for preparing Form 10-K, revised Jan. 28, 1954.

High for Any Year Included in Study
(Rounded Data)

	Highest Paid Officer	Total for Top 3
Aluminum Company of America	$2,000	$6,000
Anaconda Company	1,000	3,000
General Electric	less than $1,000	3,000 Est.
Tidewater Associated Oil	3,000	6,000

It may be fairly concluded from the tabulation that the economic benefits derived from group life insurance, while of distinct value to the individual executive, do not bulk large compared to most other benefits included in the top executive pay package.[3] However, although usually not large in amount, employer contributions for group insurance do in effect typically result in additional tax-free income for the executive.

In Chapter IV, we considered stock option and purchase gains. There is a closely allied but perhaps more debatable gain which arises when subscription rights to stock or debentures are given to employees to buy new securities at a price below the prevailing market price, but where the same opportunity is open to all company stockholders.

Whether such transactions have usually been reported to the FTC or SEC in connection with the pay of top officers seems doubtful. In any event only three such instances—involving International Paper, Phillips Petroleum, and Standard Oil (Indi-

3. For an intensive analysis of death benefits for executives see Harland Fox, "Executive Death Benefits," *Executive Benefits and Fringes,* reprinted from *Management Record* (National Industrial Conference Board, 1958).

Among companies having either group life insurance or combination plans providing for both group life insurance and annuities, several firms have reported to SEC the nature of the death benefits and contributions. Under a plan in effect during the 1940's, Socony provided a maximum death benefit for executives of $20,000 toward which the employee contributed $120 per year, the company paying the balance. Texaco had a plan effective in April, 1950, providing for a death benefit of 150 per cent of annual pay, but not more than $40,000. The employee contributed $192 per year toward this, with the company financing the rest of the cost. And in January, 1951, Tidewater Associated Oil's management group life insurance plan provided for a death benefit ranging from a minimum of $10,000 up to three times the executive's base salary, with the company footing half the cost.

ana)—have been found in the present study. We did not include the estimated gains on these transactions in the stock option and purchase totals discussed earlier.

In the case of International Paper, the average of the yearly high and low was used against the subscription price. Although not as accurate as using the market price at the time of acquisition of the security, the calculation still serves to indicate in a general way the size of the gains. For instance, the average of the high and low for 1929 for the Class C Common was $17.94. The subscription price to shareholders was $10.14. Thus there was an apparent gain of $7.80 per share. For the company's highest paid officer this gain, on 78,500 shares, amounted to $612.3 thousand, making a total for the three top officers of $683.8 thousand (one of the three had no gain).

These gains would be fully taxable along with other current income elements. The calculations assume that the stock is resold at the average market price or higher. This is consistent with the estimates made earlier in the study for stock option gains.

In the second case, Phillips Petroleum in 1957 offered to employees, including officers, the opportunity to subscribe for debentures at the subscription price to stockholders. The number of debentures of $100 par value purchased by the three top executives ranged from 4,408 for the number one man down to 1,087 for the third officer. The average market price, on the basis of the proxy data, was about $108.56, a gain over the subscription price (apparently the $100 par value) of $8.56 per $100 of debentures. This meant gains ranging from $37.7 thousand to $9.3 thousand for each of the top three, or a total of $58.7 thousand. These gains, analogous to stock option gains, would be taxable at long-term capital gains rates, assuming the debentures were held at least six months.

In a similar offering in 1952, Standard Oil (Indiana) gave officers and key employees a chance to subscribe to debentures at $100 when the market price on a when-issued basis was $106.50, or a gain of $6.50 per debenture. This resulted in unrealized capital gains of $26.7 thousand for the top three men, again subject to the capital gains tax.

The magnitude of the before-tax gains for the three top officers together indicated in each of the foregoing instances—$684 thousand, $59 thousand, and $27 thousand—suggest that such gains, while apparently few in number, certainly represent a significant element of income when they do occur. They have nonetheless been exluded from the total pay package, because the reporting of these gains to government regulatory agencies does not appear to have been complete or consistent for all companies over the 1929–1958 period.

The so-called management trust, yet another form of executive compensation not adequately reported, has not been in vogue in recent years. As indicated earlier, however, management trusts have been used in connection with stock purchase or bonus schemes benefiting the top officers of many corporations.[4] Devices of this nature have been evident in the past at GM, Du Pont, Chrysler, and other firms. Although it would be difficult if not impossible to compute the actual benefits received under management trusts from the published evidence, it is pertinent to examine the working of the device.

We take for illustration the Executive Chrysler Management Trust, which originated in 1936 and ended in 1945.[5] Abstracting from the 20 pages of legal terminology in the trust indenture, we can point out the important features:

1. A trust was formed with five trustees, one of whom was also a beneficiary of the trust.

2. The corporation agreed to lend the trustees $551,000 at 1 ½ per cent interest per year. This debt was payable Dec. 31, 1943.

3. The trustees were given the right to buy from the corporation 18,000 shares of Chrysler common for $34.10 per share or $613,800 in total.

4. See Chapter IV, p. 84.
5. *Executive Chrysler Management Trust,* indenture August 11, 1936.

4. The corporation would pay to the trustees (after deducting 7 per cent of capital and surplus) the following fractions of net earnings after taxes and certain other charges:

1936–38	0%	1941	.32%
1939	.11	1942	.43
1940	.22	1943–45	.54

5. Beneficiaries of the trust fund would pay $7 a share in cash for a total of 9,000 shares of beneficial interest in the trust.

6. The $63,000 from the beneficiaries plus the $551,000 loan from the corporation would pay for the stock.

7. Dividends on the stock and company profit contributions were expected to be the principal sources of income to the trust.

8. The income was to be used first to pay any necessary expenses of administration of the trust, including payments of interest and principal on the loan from the corporation.

9. Any income remaining after expenses generally would be either reinvested in more Chrysler common, or distributed to the beneficiaries at least yearly either in cash or in stock.

10. The trust was to be distributed as to not more than one-third of the principal at the end of 1943. Up to one-half of the remainder was to be passed out at the end of 1944 and the rest at the end of 1945.

11. Yearly income distributions and final distributions of principal were to be prorated according to the shares of beneficial interest held by each executive covered.

In the light of the foregoing provisions, it is interesting to observe the sparseness of detailed evidence in the SEC records. On one point, however, the records are quite revealing: the 9,000 shares of beneficial interest were held entirely by three Chrysler executives, each having 3,000 shares. In short, each of these officers would get a third of the income and a third of the principal, barring early retirement, death, and so forth.

The records also indicate something of the final distribution of principal to each officer: In 1945, $175 thousand ($10 thousand in cash); in 1946, $11.8 thousand; in 1947, $79.7 thousand. The SEC records show nothing about benefits received in 1937 or 1942, however, the years with which we were concerned.

The management trust device in general is significant because its financial complexity, shrouded in legal verbiage, has had the effect of concealing from the general public much of the compensation accruing to top executives in the largest corporations, at least in earlier years. These and other efforts at concealment had, of course, a substantial effect in awakening the public to the need for more adequate reporting of executive compensation. The efforts of the FTC and later the SEC have not only resulted in more adequate reporting of such payments, but appear to have eliminated the management trust, at least in the form just described, as a substantial factor in executive compensation.

Nevertheless in the present study there is still undoubtedly some understatement, especially for 1929, in calculation of stock purchase gains and bonuses, and in the total pay package as a result of the use of such devices. There is, however, no real way of knowing the extent of this understatement.

Aside from insurance, stock and debenture subscription gains, and benefits from management trusts, other items of compensation in the partially reported or difficult-to-measure category appear occasionally in SEC records. An interesting example is the employment contract made between the American Smelting and Refining Company and one of its vice-presidents in 1936. It includes a type of provision not often seen. In addition to being assured of a yearly salary of $75,000, the vice-president was told:

You are to be entitled to participate in any mining venture undertaken by the company during the period of your employment, to the extent of a maximum of three percent of the company's interest. By "participation" is meant that you are to pay your percentage of the money invested in such mining enterprise contemporaneously with payment of its part by the undersigned company.

Election of your desire to participate in any venture must be made at the time the company undertakes that venture. . . .[6]

Elements Not Reported—Expense Accounts

In an entirely different category from the partially reported or difficult-to-measure pay elements are executive expense accounts. Such accounts have never been reported in the information submitted to government regulatory bodies.[7] Despite the absence of reporting, we can still look at the conflicting labor and management views on expense accounts as an income factor, the relation of taxes to expense account abuses, what is actually included in expense accounts, how these accounts can be considered differently from an economic as contrasted with a tax viewpoint, and, finally, the three types of income that accrue to top executives in connection with expense accounts.

Labor and management spokesmen have made clear radically different attitudes with regard to the expense accounts of top executives. Labor has been critical. For example, in a recent speech before a group of business executives Albert J. Hayes, president of the International Association of Machinists and a vice-president of AFL-CIO, pointed to "management featherbedding" in the form of "surplus vice presidents, managers, and directors." He also pointed to a second form of featherbedding consisting of payments made

through such devices as inflated expense accounts, stock options, bonuses, country-club memberships and company-paid yacht cruises and hunting trips. . . .

6. American Smelting and Refining Company, Form 8-K, January 11, 1937, Exhibit C.

7. The one exception found in our study was the 1929 report to the FTC by International Paper Company which revealed that the company's top executive in that year received in addition to substantial option gains and $60,000 in salary an amount of $20,000 labeled "expenses."

These items cost American industry a staggering sum and one that is growing each year.[8]

In sharp contrast to the critical view of labor is the attitude of management. Some top executives tend to slough off the criticism; others acknowledge it but appear to feel little need for any change in company policies.

Reflective of the former attitude on the part of the executives surveyed is the report of one writer, Challis A. Hall, Jr., who investigated the differing types of executive compensation plans in the early post-World War II years:

According to executives interviewed, company-paid-for expenses of the type which really reduce executives' living costs and represent extra income are of negligible importance in large companies.[9]

On the other hand, an executive responding to another survey had this to say:

I don't like the idea of a corporation assuming a lot of expenses that are of a somewhat questionable nature, many of them semi-personal. This breeds laxity, lack of discipline, and disorderly procedure. Admittedly, the problem with top and junior executives on items of expense of this nature is that they are paying for them with very cheap dollars. Our present tax situation leaves no alternative but to do some of these things, but it is a pity it got so far out of hand.[10]

Even though executive expense accounts do not appear to be of particularly recent origin, it would seem that their use as a mechanism for tax avoidance (or evasion) is directly related to the level of the federal corporate income and excess profits taxes. In the years before 1940, the federal corporate income tax rates, never more than 15 per cent,[11] meant that a dollar of corporate

8. "Management Tied to Featherbedding," *New York Times,* May 19, 1960.
9. Challis A. Hall, Jr., *Effects of Taxation—Executive Compensation and Retirement Plans* (Boston: Graduate School of Business Administration, Harvard University, 1951), p. 14.
10. Malcolm G. Neuhoff, *Executive Expense Accounts,* Studies in Business Policy, No. 67 (New York: National Industrial Conference Board, 1954), p. 5.
11. William H. Husband and James C. Dockeray, *Modern Corporation Finance* (Homewood, Illinois: Richard D. Irwin, 1957), 4th ed., p. 733.

profits after taxes was still worth 85 cents, only 15 cents going to the government. This was not a "cheap" dollar. In World War II, however, the rate of 95 per cent imposed on excess profits meant that 95 cents out of every such dollar went to the U.S. Treasury and only five cents remained with the corporation. After the war when the rate dropped to 38 per cent the dollar became more expensive at 62 cents. But in 1950–1951 the rates climbed again with a new excess profits tax marginal rate of 77 per cent, and the extra dollar was reduced in value to 23 cents. In more recent years, the 52 per cent corporate tax rate has meant that each after-tax dollar is thought of as being worth 48 cents. These are still regarded as cheap dollars.

As to the impact of these cheap dollars, one tax specialist, Beardsley Ruml, stated in 1951 when the marginal rate was 77 per cent:

In essence, what has happened is that for some companies, cheap dollars have been created which make prudent the taking of risks that would be considered doubtful if all expense dollars had the same value.

He even went on to urge "that the payment of an excess profits tax by a company in 1952 gives a presumption of managerial inadequacy."[12]

The implication appears to have been that, if the marginal dollars were worth only 23 cents, they might as well be spent by the company in almost any way it saw fit, rather than become excess profits and go mostly to the government. And there can be no question but that this type of spending favored laxity in regard to executive expense accounts.

While the corporate tax is now below the Korean War level, it would appear that "cheap dollar" thinking about executive expense accounts still dominates management's attitude, at least in some circles. A fact which tends to reinforce such thinking is that expenses can be made tax-free to the executive

12. Beardsley Ruml, "Management under the Excess Profits Tax," Address before the 15th Annual Meeting of the Gas Appliance Manufacturers Association, Chicago, April 17, 1951, pp. 11, 12.

at a time when his other compensation is typically subject either to high individual income tax rates or to capital gains rates.

With regard to the effect of the corporate income tax an article in one periodical had this pungent statement from a member of Congress: "I think if it were possible to cut our corporation tax down to around 30% again you'd have a lot of moaning in all the night clubs."[13]

For purposes of analysis, we include in the executive expense account category certain expenses of a corporation which are tied in closely with the activities of individual executives. These expenses can be broken down roughly into travel expenses, entertainment expenses, club memberships, and the use of special facilities.

Travel expenses typically include the cost of out-of-town trips which involve transportation, lodging, meals, often some entertainment, and lesser expenses. Whether the travel expenses of an executive's wife should be paid for by the company is often a problem. Entertainment expense may mean the cost of theater tickets, night-club expenses, attendance at sports events, and in certain cases entertainment at the executive's home. Club memberships can vary all the way from technical and trade associations to social and athletic clubs. Problems of allocating the expense for the latter can be more vexing to the executive. Under special facilities made available to executives, can be listed company-subsidized lunch rooms, hotel suites, farms, hunting lodges, cars, yachts, and airplanes.

Expense accounts can be regarded as giving an income benefit to executives in two quite different ways. For example, if the company should reimburse an executive for what is really personal entertainment expense, this could be regarded both as economic income to the executive and as income from the point of view of taxes. By contrast, the more expensive hotel accommodations given to a company president compared to those furnished the average employee probably will not mean any added

13. "Expense Accounts: A $5 Billion Tax Deduction, and Growing," *U.S. News and World Report,* August 16, 1957, p. 86.

income from a tax viewpoint. But from an economic standpoint, the difference in cost of accommodations can be regarded as income to the executive.

In addition to consideration from an economic versus a tax viewpoint, executive expenses can be classed according to the nature of the income. There may be excess of expense allowance over actual expense; expense excess over normal business expense arising out of status considerations; or personal expense reimbursed as business expense.

In certain cases, a company pays an executive an expense allowance, out of which he is expected to defray certain entertainment and other expenses related to the business, without being obliged to render an accounting of the actual expenses to his company. If the amount of the allowance exceeds the amount actually spent by the executive during the year, the difference is really income. It is economic income, and it must be reported on the executive's federal income tax return.

The Internal Revenue Service has recently placed greater emphasis on this point. Expense account allowances must now be reported on the company's corporate income tax return for each of its 25 highest paid officers earning in excess of $10,000 (including the amount of the allowance). Where the executive is not required to account to his employer for his business expenses, he must do so on his personal income tax return.[14]

There are certain expenses for travel, entertainment, and so forth, which involve extra expense over normal business expense due to the status of the executive. The excess can be regarded as economic income, as in our example of expensive hotel accommodations, but it is not necessarily income from a tax viewpoint. That such expense, which we shall simply call "status expense," is usual among the top executives of the larger companies can be confirmed from Neuhoff:

14. U.S. Internal Revenue Service, official statement on entertainment expenses and employees' expense accounts, as quoted in *U.S. News and World Report,* January 11, 1960, p. 97.

Executives are usually permitted to choose their own travel accommodations, according to the companies reporting in this study. And in most cases the accommodations chosen are better than those which would be granted to the average employee. This distinction in travel accommodations is a conscious policy on the part of the companies concerned. Executives are permitted better accommodations because they are representing the company in dealings with executives of other companies, and it is felt that the accommodations should give the executive prestige. Further it is pointed out, men in higher salary brackets are accustomed to traveling, living, and eating in a better style than the average employee and should not be expected to lower their standards when traveling on company business.[15]

Sanders points out why some of this status expense is incurred in particular by company presidents:

Throughout this study much was said about the requirements of the top job—the president's position. He is a marked man; there are things that only he can do, partly because other presidents, and some who think of themselves as presidents, will deal only with him. He in particular must have the facilities by which, and in which, that kind of business can be transacted. He must live commensurately with his position at his home, his office, and his club. This is not merely for pomp and circumstance, but still more for convenience, for being sequestered where important business can be privately transacted and for meeting with others on equal terms.[16]

Status expense is exemplified in each of the following types of difference: bedrooms on trains vs. roomettes or lower berths; use of a full-time or part-time chauffeur with a company car;[17] higher mileage allowance for larger cars, where executives drive their own; suites in hotels vs. bedrooms; where travel is per diem, a higher per diem for top executives; for companies owning airplanes, the excess cost per passenger on the company plane as

15. Neuhoff, *op. cit.,* p. 6.
16. Thomas H. Sanders, *Effects of Taxation on Executives* (Boston: Graduate School of Business Administration, Harvard University, 1951), p. 151.
17. One survey even revealed that in two firms the chief executive was given two cars, one for business and the other for personal use. This was reported in Nicholas L. A. Martucci, "Executive Extras," in *Executive Benefits and Fringes,* reprinted from *Management Record* (New York: National Industrial Conference Board, 1958), p. 22.

against an airline ticket; for other companies, first-class vs. tourist airline tickets.

To what degree status expense is necessary business expense and how much just high living, is a question that is difficult to answer. It is enough here to point out that, from an economic viewpoint, such expense can be regarded as a form of income to the executive. From a tax viewpoint, it is important only insofar as it may raise an executive's total expense account to a level that would be disproportionate in relation to his income and occupation. As the Internal Revenue Service has stated:

The field offices have also been advised to pay particular attention to the examination of returns in which the deductions claimed for entertainment and similar expenses appear to be disproportionate in relationship to the income and business activities of the taxpayer.[18]

The most obvious type of income resulting from expense accounts comes from what is really personal expense, which is reimbursed as business expense. Such expense is not only economic income, it is also taxable. On items for which there may be a reasonable doubt, Sanders has suggested the following standards: (1) Should the expenditure be made at all (that is, does it pay for itself in the business sense)? (2) Should the expenditure incurred by the employee be borne by the employee or by the company (is it personal or is it business)?[19]

Certain expense items which have troubled (or are likely to trouble) top executives can be considered in the light of these standards. This category includes, as we have suggested, the question of credit cards, club membership, entertainment expenses, and company airplanes.

While some credit cards are limited in scope, permitting only certain types of charges—rides on any airline for an airline credit card, or items purchasable at service stations for an oil company credit card—others cover a wider range of activities. One firm which issues credit cards, for example, advertizes world-

18. U.S. Internal Revenue Service, *op. cit.*, p. 98.
19. Sanders, *op. cit.*, p. 147.

wide charge services, including restaurants; hotels and motels; night clubs; transportation via air, rail, bus, and steamship; tours and cruises; auto rentals, gasoline, and automobile repair services; gift and florist shop purchases; liquor; overseas cables; and other services.

To the extent that personal bills are paid for by the company, this constitutes both economic and taxable income to the executive, since the use of a credit card does not, of course, establish the outlay as a business expense. However, the fact that the company is furnished with a bill can help to establish that an expense was incurred.

As to executive expenses involving clubs, few questions arise in regard to trade or technical associations where the relation to business is clear. But for social or athletic clubs, personal expense can easily be charged off to the company as business expense, giving rise to both economic and taxable income.

Martucci had this to say in one survey of executive expenses: "All companies report that they pay initiation fees and membership dues in full . . . but charges of a personal nature are borne by the individual executive."[20] Actually, it would appear that, unless all costs are truly business expense, there arises both economic and taxable income to the executive in the case of part of the dues and initiation fees. A more honest way of allocating expenses would be to prorate the dues according to the proportions of business and personal expense. The same might be done for the initiation fees on the basis of the first year's club expenses.

In the matter of entertainment, there can be little doubt that as to the amounts of money involved, it accounts for a large share of the expense account totals. Both from an economic and tax viewpoint whatever is really personal rather than business expense is income. On the tax angle one authority has indicated:

Business entertainment can qualify as an ordinary and necessary business expense; however . . . the taxpayer should be prepared to show the amount so spent, who was entertained, and the connection between those enter-

20. Martucci, *op. cit.*, p. 24.

tained and the taxpayer's business. The connection must not be too remote. The person entertained should be a customer, a potential customer, a person able to influence potential customers, or a person otherwise able to render material service to the taxpayer, and the amount of the expense in each case should be reasonable in relation to the benefit expected.[21]

A marginal type of entertainment expense is at-home entertainment. One company reporting on this subject in the Martucci survey stated: "We limit such entertainment to U.S. Government representatives and foreign diplomats."[22] The theory behind this approach to getting government business is an interesting subject for speculation. Is it the idea that you use entertainment to get government business in the same way you do any other business, and that the at-home provision makes certain that the executive is not out-of-pocket on this account? Or is there a policy of barring such entertainment in public, but encouraging it so long as it is done in private?

It seems to be implied in the quotation from the Martucci survey above that the Internal Revenue Service has in some cases followed a policy of allowing a corporate income tax deduction for the cost of entertainment of government officials. At the same time, responsible administrators in other branches of the federal government have stressed that government officials should not accept entertainment by business firms, since their policy decisions might be swayed by considerations other than the public interest. This apparent inconsistency in government policy certainly merits further investigation.

It is of note that, in the new questions regarding expense accounts that have been added to the corporate income tax return, inquiries are made about hunting lodges and about yachts, but there has been as yet no mention of company airplanes. It is difficult to understand why they have not been included. The fact is that many of the largest companies have their own aircraft, and some of them even operate fleets of airplanes.

21. *Federal Taxes, 1958* (New York and other: Commerce Clearing House, 1958), p. 421.
22. Martucci, *op. cit.*, p. 27.

110

The facts on costs and other aspects of company-owned aircraft have been explored in a study by this writer and Neuhoff covering 131 companies.[23] The study revealed, among other things, that yearly costs of operation in 1952, for the most widely used single-engine aircraft,[24] were around $15,000, but for twin-engine planes annual costs were on the order of $50 to $100 thousand.

On the use of company planes, the survey concluded that "most companies cooperating in this study indicate that their planes are provided primarily for the use of members of top management."[25] The use of the larger corporate aircraft more or less exclusively by top management suggests that the planes are often employed, not solely for transportation, but also as a means of conferring a tax-free benefit on the top executives. Accordingly, it is appropriate to treat company airplane expense in much the same way as other expense account items.

We have already mentioned the status expense incurred through company airplanes. This, of course, constitutes an element of economic income. But the more important point with regard to company airplanes is the one raised by Sanders' question: does it pay for itself in the business sense?

Take the case of a top company salesman who is given an airplane ride up to the north woods to go hunting and fishing as a special incentive for outstanding sales performance. The company can point to the sales volume in justification of the expense. Another example would be flying a key specialist to a company plant in order to prevent the shutdown of a production line in an emergency. The company can point to the costs which might otherwise be incurred. Most flights probably depend,

23. Leonard R. Burgess and Malcolm C. Neuhoff, *Managing Company Airplanes,* Studies in Business Policy No. 65 (New York: National Industrial Conference Board, 1954).

24. Single-engine aircraft are often used for what are obviously business purposes, such as pipeline patrol by oil companies. For cost data see Burgess and Neuhoff, *op. cit.,* p. 10.

25. *Ibid.,* p. 20.

111

however, for their justification on the saving in travel time for top executives.

From a tax viewpoint, income to the executive may be recognized, if a flight is really for personal rather than for business purposes. This would, for example, prohibit deduction on the corporation's tax return for expenses incurred by an officer in commuting to and from work, or for a vacation trip. Of course, aside from personal use, the Internal Revenue Service may in the future also question totals for individual executives when the amounts appear "disproportionate" in relation to income or job responsibility, as it already does for other types of expense account expenditures.

VI

The Total
Pay Package

Having previously discussed the executive pay package by analyzing each of its major parts in turn, we are now ready to explore the package as a whole, including not only direct payments, such as salaries and currently paid bonuses, but also major fringe benefits including deferred bonuses, various post-retirement benefits, and stock option gains. To discover the important trends in the total pay of executives in the period 1929–1958, the major pay elements, reclassified according to the economically more significant nature and extent of deferment, will be analyzed both in terms of the over-all totals for the 25-company sample and on the basis of the performance of individual companies.

The 25-Company Totals

The total pay package for all three top executives in all of the 25 largest manufacturing companies in 1958 was more than $20 million before taxes and more than $10.7 million after taxes. How figures of such magnitude are judged varies with the measure used. Viewed in terms of financial ratios, the figures are not large. For example, using the 21 out of the 25 companies which reported payroll information in *Moody's Industrials,* the before-tax total in 1958 was only a little over .12 per cent of payroll—including in most cases wages, salaries, and related employment costs. Another way of looking at the $20 million is that it represents the total pay package for 75 executives, or $268,000 per executive before taxes. The corresponding figure after taxes is $142,000. When the data are viewed this way, judgment is likely to be a function of income level. The employee lower down in the organization is apt to regard the top executive's pay, either before or after taxes, as large, while the executive himself may think the opposite. A third way of measuring, which we shall also use, is to look at the composition of the pay package in terms of its major elements.

The average pay, including major fringes, for the three highest paid executives taken together in the 25 largest manufacturing companies is shown by the top solid line in Diagram 15. The solid line below it shows the average after taxes. A third, dashed line shows the real after-tax average and reflects a cost of living adjustment. The adjusted line was obtained by dividing the after-tax average by the BLS consumer price index, rebased to 1929 = 100.[1] The diagram makes evident that the net move-

1. The index actually measures changes in the prices of goods and services purchased by city wage-earner and clerical-worker families to maintain their level of living. Accordingly an argument can be made that it is not appropriate for use in measuring the cost of living for top executives. Also, over a three-decade period the validity of such an index is much less than would be the case for a shorter period. See Frederick C. Mills, *Statistical Methods* (New York: Henry Holt, 1955), 3rd ed., pp. 463, 472.

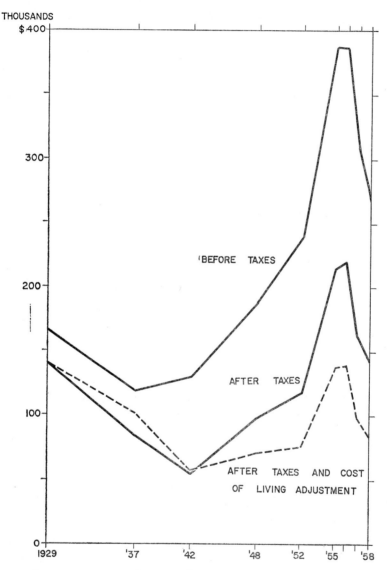

THOUSANDS

$400

300

200

100

0

BEFORE TAXES

AFTER TAXES

AFTER TAXES AND COST
OF LIVING ADJUSTMENT

1929   '37   '42   '48   '52   '55   '58

Diagram 15—Trends in Total Pay, Average of Top Three

1 1 5

ment before taxes of the average pay of the top executive was from $166,000 in 1929 to $268,000 in 1958, a rise of more than 60 per cent; the net movement after taxes was only from $140,000 to 142,000, or barely any increase at all; and the movement after taxes and an adjustment for cost of living was from $140,000 to $84,000, or a decrease of 40 per cent. The overall movement can be broken down into two major periods: first, the decline until 1937 (1942 after taxes); second, the advance that took place thereafter. This secondary advance could prove more representative of the trend than the apparent longer run trends mentioned above because of future exercise of stock options already granted.

It is difficult to make accurate comparisons with pay movements for other groups in the economy. Data for leaders in various professional occupations, for example, suffer from a lag in publication. However, the figures for 1929 and 1952, though not inclusive of major fringes, strongly suggest that the pay of professional persons has advanced more rapidly than that for top executives. The data show that, compared to an increase of about 43 per cent in top executive pay for the 25 largest companies, pay of college teachers rose 67 per cent, that of lawyers 63 per cent, that of physicians 157 per cent and that of engineers 179 per cent.[2] Percentage increases of this nature do not, of course, reflect the actual levels of pay. In the case of college teachers, for example, the increase was from an extremely low level.

The peaks of 1955–1956, evident in all three of the lines in the diagram, were caused by the heavy exercise of stock options during those years. The remaining years since 1952 are

2. Data are not altogether comparable for various reasons. The top executive figure includes major fringes while the others do not. The data for teachers are based on average annual salary, while those for lawyers and physicians are based on average annual net income, and those for engineers are determined from median base monthly salary rates. The more recent figure for physicians is for 1951, while that for engineers is for 1953 and includes graduate engineers only while the 1929 figure includes nongraduates as well. Data are taken from U.S. Department of Commerce, Bureau of the Census, *Historical Statistics of the U.S., Colonial Times to 1957* (Washington: U.S. Government Printing Office, 1960), Series D 728–734, p. 97.

higher than they otherwise would be because of stock option gains. The 1958 option gains in the averages were not large compared to other years, but they can be discounted in part because of the recession. The future exercise of options already granted may in fact tend to boost the averages shown, forcing the trends upward, even to the extent of reversing the apparently less rapid rise in executive compensation in comparison to the pay for professional groups.

From a comparison of the over-all trends in the total, or average pay package, of the top officer, we now turn to an analysis of the trends and percentage relationships within the pay package. In so doing it will be helpful to consider a regrouping of the pay items. In previous chapters the different items of the pay package were treated in some detail according to the type of payment—currently paid bonuses, pension benefits, thrift plan benefits, and so forth. This method of classification, while useful from the viewpoint of personnel administration, is not the most significant one from an economic standpoint. In this respect it is also valuable to examine the pay package of the top executive with its contents classified by the extent of deferment. For example, there is little difference economically between currently paid cash and stock bonuses, and salaries and fees, which are also paid currently.

Regrouping of the pay items before taxes for the three top officers taken together for all 25 manufacturing companies in 1958 is shown in Diagram 16. The black boxes on the left represent the pay items by type of payment, while the white boxes on the right show the elements regrouped by the extent of deferment. The two lowest black boxes, salaries and fees, and currently paid bonuses, are grouped together as being both currently paid. Short-term deferred cash and stock bonuses are reclassified as short-term deferment. Income values of thrift plan benefits, deferred cash payments under contract, pension benefits, and postretirement cash and stock bonuses are regrouped to form the single category of postretirement deferment. Stock option and purchase gains are recast as flexible deferment.

117

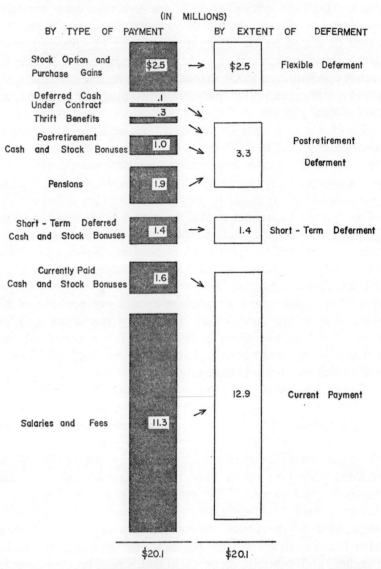

(IN MILLIONS)

BY TYPE OF PAYMENT   BY EXTENT OF DEFERMENT

Stock Option and Purchase Gains $2.5   → $2.5   Flexible Deferment

Deferred Cash Under Contract   .1
Thrift Benefits   .3

Postretirement Cash and Stock Bonuses   1.0   3.3   Postretirement Deferment

Pensions   1.9

Short - Term Deferred Cash and Stock Bonuses   1.4   →   1.4   Short - Term Deferment

Currently Paid Cash and Stock Bonuses   1.6

Salaries and Fees   11.3   12.9   Current Payment

$20.1 $20.1

Diagram 16—Total Pay Before Taxes in 1958, Top Three Together

118

The new grouping of pay package elements can be seen in action in Diagrams 17, 18, 19, and 20. The first two trace the rates of advance of the key elements in the pay package before and after taxes, while the others indicate the percentage make-up of the total.

In Diagrams 17 and 18, the general arrangement of the lines is similar. The uppermost line represents the movement of the total pay package. Next comes the line for current payment. The solid line underneath that is for postretirement deferment. The dashed line is for short-term deferment, and the bottom line represents the element of flexible deferment. From these two diagrams it is clear that, both before and after taxes, current payment showed less percentage movement either up or down than any other pay element. Moreover, a difference in trend between the two lines is evident. The before-taxes line for current payment undulated gently, ending up in 1958 at a level slightly ahead of 1929. The after-taxes line showed more movement. It fell until 1942 and, despite some recovery, was, in 1958, still below the 1929 level.

Before taxes, there appears to have been a race between short-term and postretirement deferment, with the latter apparently beginning to come out on top just in the last three years. After taxes, the same rivalry is apparent, but a shifting in favor of postretirement deferment seems to have taken place as early as 1942.

Flexible deferment is by far the most volatile element in the pay package, viewed either before or after taxes. Before taxes it dropped from 1929 to 1937, disappeared thereafter, reappearing in 1948, in 1955 and 1956 rising above all other pay elements except current payment, and dropping again after that. After taxes the flexible deferment curve behaved much the same as before taxes, except in the two years 1955 and 1956, when it exceeded even current payment.

The percentage make-up of the total pay package before and after taxes for the top three executives taken together for all

119

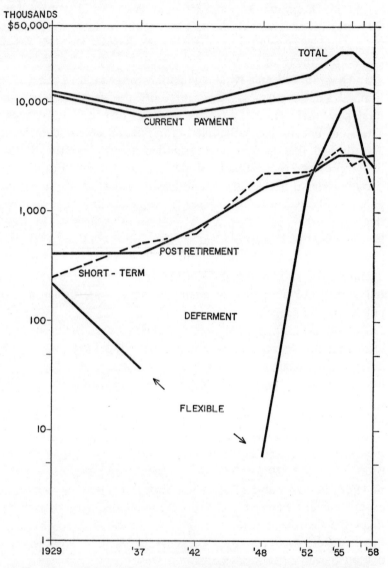

THOUSANDS
$50,000

TOTAL

10,000

CURRENT PAYMENT

1,000

POST RETIREMENT

SHORT - TERM

100

DEFERMENT

FLEXIBLE

10

1
1929   '37   '42   '48   '52 '55 '58

Diagram 17—Pay Elements Before Taxes, Top Three Together

120

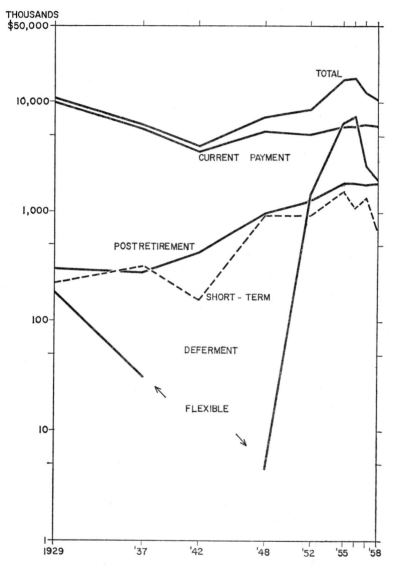

THOUSANDS
$50,000

TOTAL

10,000

CURRENT PAYMENT

1,000

POST RETIREMENT

SHORT - TERM

100

DEFERMENT

FLEXIBLE

10

1

1929   '37   '42   '48   '52   '55   '58

Diagram 18—Pay Elements After Taxes, Top Three Together

121

25 companies in the sample is shown in Diagrams 19 and 20. It may be concluded from the diagrams that current payment in the 1929–1958 period dropped from over 93 per cent to 64 per cent of the total pay package, viewed before taxes. After taxes, the drop was from 93 per cent to 59 per cent. Deferred payment in all its different forms increased, before taxes, from less than 7 per cent to 36 per cent. The after-tax rise ended at 41 per cent. In the years 1955–1957 the shifts appeared even more pronounced, because of the ballooning of flexible deferment. Although the balloon seems to have deflated somewhat, flexible deferment in 1958 still accounted for 13 per cent of the total pay package (18 per cent after taxes), compared to less than 2 per cent back in 1929. Short-term deferment had its vacillations as a percentage of the total, but was much steadier in performance than flexible deferment. Only 2 per cent in 1929, it rose to claim over 7 per cent of the total pay package in 1958, before taxes. The 1958 figure after taxes was 6 per cent. Except for a temporary relapse in 1955–1956, post-retirement deferment occupied a continually widening sector, growing from a little over 3 per cent before taxes in 1929 to well over 16 per cent in 1958. After taxes, the climb was from less than 3 per cent to more than 17 per cent.

Performance of Individual Companies

Although the main interest in our study attaches to totals for the 25-company sample, the performance of the individual firm merits attention. There have been significant developments in the total pay package for the three highest paid officers in terms of the individual concern. A brief review of historical developments for each year included in the 25-company sample will serve to reveal some of the threads of change in the fabric of individual company pay packages. For this purpose we revert again to the type-of-payment method of classifying pay items.

1 2 2

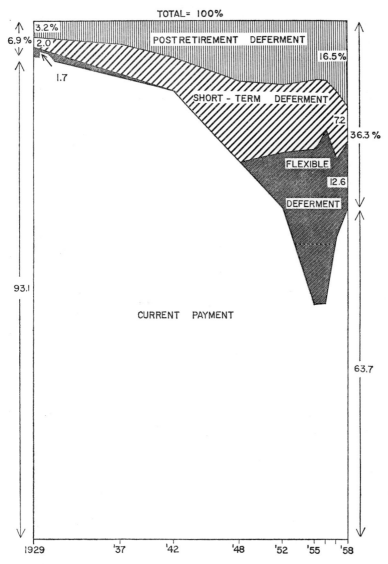

TOTAL= 100%

3.2%
6.9%
2.0
1.7

POST RETIREMENT   DEFERMENT
16.5%

SHORT - TERM   DEFERMENT
7.2
36.3 %

FLEXIBLE
12.6

DEFERMENT

CURRENT   PAYMENT

93.1

63.7

1929   '37   '42   '48   '52   '55   '58

Diagram 19—Total Pay Package Before Taxes, Top Three Together

123

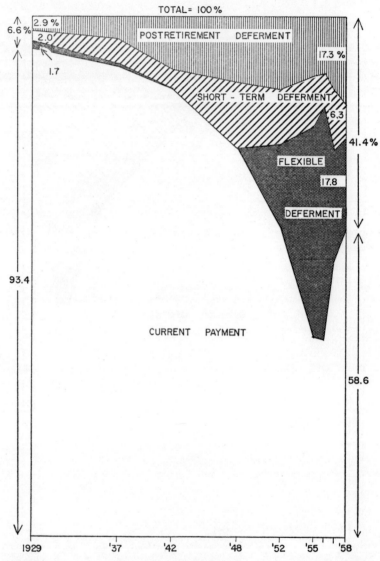

Diagram 20—Total Pay Package After Taxes, Top Three Together

124

In 1929 the pay package, as indicated in the FTC data, was heavily concentrated in salary and in current cash and stock bonus payments. Savings and thrift plan benefits were represented by a single firm in Shell Oil's provident fund. A bonus payable over the years following the award appeared only in the case of Du Pont's B Bonus. Only one company reported a stock option gain—International Paper—and it applied to a single executive and was fully taxable. Pensions, a small item in size, nevertheless showed up for the top three officers in 15 out of the 25 companies in the sample. While benefits from stock purchase and option schemes may have been underreported in the FTC data, such gains were illusory, as we pointed out in Chapter IV.

Out of the 25 firms sampled, 13 paid their top executives a current bonus in either cash or stock. A look at the totals indicates that such bonuses exceeded salary payments by a thin margin. Excluding the Bethlehem Steel figures, however, would show salaries running ahead of current bonus payments.

Inquiries at the FTC and other evidence[3] point to the fact that the presidents of two of the largest companies, Standard Oil (New Jersey) and Du Pont, were not included in the three highest paid, apparently since they were paid a salary but no bonus. This was also true of the chairman of the board of Bethlehem Steel, but not of its president.

Another feature of the 1929 picture is the relatively light impact of the individual income tax. Thus where complex pay devices existed in 1929, causes other than tax avoidance were operative.

For 1937 the plethora of firms having current cash and stock bonuses dwindled to only five companies. Stock option gains showed up for one firm, but not the same company as in 1929. Standard Oil (Indiana) and Standard Oil (New Jersey) joined Shell Oil in showing thrift plan benefits. Two companies, Du Pont and GM, reported cash and stock bonuses payable over the years following the award. There was no change in the num-

3. For further comment on this subject see John C. Baker, *Executive Salaries and Bonus Plans* (New York and London: McGraw-Hill, 1938), pp. 203, 247.

ber of companies reporting payment of pension benefits to any of their three top officers. And there were no indications of postretirement benefits (excluding thrift benefits) other than pensions.

Not only did the number of companies reporting current bonus payments drop, but the amounts were abruptly reduced compared to 1929. The oil industry in particular showed this change, no oil company reporting a bonus in 1937. In addition, the tax effect on the pay package was more noticeable in 1937.

The salient features of pay in 1942 reflected wartime pressures. Salaries ran at levels only slightly above those for 1937. Bonuses were reported by only eight companies, and two of these apparently paid a bonus to only one of their top three men.

Only one thrift plan, that of Shell, appeared to be fully operative, undoubtedly because of a shift by many firms to the purchase of war bonds. Two companies, GM and Du Pont, reported cash and stock bonuses payable following the year of award. Stock option gains disappeared. A big increase was shown in the number of companies giving pension benefits to the top men—22 out of the 25 companies covered.

The penetrating effect of wartime taxes was clear, with compensation after taxes usually being cut more than half. Typically, allowable deductions were a smaller part of gross income than in earlier years.

In 1948 new items began to appear in the pay package. Postretirement stock benefits appeared for the first time with the GE plan. Deferred cash payments under contract showed up for two companies—Gulf Oil and U.S. Steel. Stock purchase and option gains reappeared with Union Carbide's stock purchase plan coming into operation. Only two concerns, Shell and Standard Oil (New Jersey), showed thrift plan benefits, and the amounts were greater than during the war. Although there was no change in the number of companies providing pension benefits, the income values were higher. A bonus deferred over the years following award was reported by three companies—

Gulf Oil, Du Pont, and GM. Six firms showed current bonuses.

Over all, a shift toward deferred benefits was evident. Behind this shift would appear to be an increased consciousness of the impact of taxation, which remained heavy, despite some lowering of rates from the wartime highs.

In 1952 stock option and purchase gains entered the picture more strongly, three concerns reporting such income—Goodyear, Union Carbide, and Phillips Petroleum. Current bonuses in stock or cash were reported by six firms—International Harvester, Goodyear, Westinghouse, Bethlehem Steel, GE, and American Tobacco.

Confined to the oil industry, savings and thrift plans showed an increase. Seven companies reported this type of gain: Standard Oil (New Jersey), Socony, Standard Oil (California), Texaco, Standard Oil (Indiana), Cities Service, and Shell.

Two other companies followed the pattern of GE in providing postretirement stock and cash benefits—Dow Chemical in cash (tied in with a pension plan), and Texaco with a stock distribution scheme. Four concerns, Gulf Oil, GM, Du Pont, and Chrysler, reported bonuses payable over the years following the award. Gulf Oil and Chrysler, in addition to U.S. Steel, provided deferred cash payments under contract to one or more of their top officers. Finally pension plan benefits had increased to the point where only one of the 25 largest companies (Anaconda Copper) did not yet provide its top officers with benefits under a formalized pension plan.

Regardless of a growing trend to option and thrift plans, taking advantage of the capital gains provisions of the Internal Revenue Code, or other types of deferment intended to postpone the taking of income to later years of supposedly lesser income, the effect of the income tax continued to be felt, somewhat more so than in 1948.

Bonus payments on a current basis, which since 1948 had remained popular with several concerns, lost support in 1955, only four companies reporting such payments to their top men.

Five concerns reported bonuses payable over the years following the award. And five others reported postretirement bonuses.

Ten firms, all in the oil industry, reported thrift and savings plan benefits. Four companies reported fixed deferred cash payments under employment contracts, going in all instances to only one or two of the senior officers. And for the first time, in 1955, all 25 companies provided pension benefits for their three top executives.

Finally and most noticeable of all, 1955 saw 11 out of 25 manufacturing companies with top officers exercising stock option or purchase privileges. Assuming in the tax calculations that stock purchased was sold after the necessary holding period and taxed at long-term capital gains rates, the options had the effect of materially increasing the after-tax income of officers exercising options. Generally an executive who previously was taxed so that he retained less than half of the pre-tax package was now able to keep 60 to 70 per cent of his pre-tax corporate income.

The tendency of bonuses paid currently to lose out continued in 1956 with only three companies, Bethlehem Steel, International Harvester, and GE, still reporting them. In the GE case this was, however, in addition to a postretirement stock distribution.

Ford, GM, Gulf Oil, and Du Pont continued to show bonuses payable over the years following award, typically over four or five years, but sometimes over a ten-year span. (Chrysler paid no bonus in 1956.) Bonuses payable after retirement in stock or cash were indicated by six concerns, four paying in stock, two in cash.

Thrift plan benefits continued strong, with a new convert outside the oil industry—GM. Deferred cash under contract was reported by only three companies, payable to only one or two executives, perhaps evidencing a slightly lessened interest in this type of compensation.

Stock option and purchase gains were reported by 13 companies, more than in 1955. The greater after-tax income as a re-

128

sult of stock option capital gains continued in the case of the many officers who exercised options.

Deferred cash payments under contract lost further support in 1957, with only two firms reporting such benefits, which went to only one executive in each concern. By contrast thrift plan benefits were reported by 11 firms, with U.S. Steel joining GM in the non-oil sector of manufacturing.

Current bonuses were reported by five companies. Six companies paid their top men bonuses over the years following the award, while six other concerns followed the GE emphasis in delaying all or part of the bonus payments until after retirement. All but one case involved stock rather than cash.

A smaller number of companies than in earlier years (nine), reported stock option and purchase gains. In each company fewer officers exercised options. As a result, the normal tax incision into the top executive pay package tended to reassert itself, with the after-tax package once more being reduced to half the pre-tax take.

A cyclical influence was noticeable in 1958. Salaries in general came to a halt in their usual year-to-year advance. In some cases they were even cut. Four companies reported currently paid bonuses, four reported them paid in the years following the year of award, and six firms continued to report post-retirement bonuses, predominantly in stock. In both 1957 and 1958 GM and Du Pont reported new devices called, respectively, contingent credits and dividend units, which would be effective to the extent stock options were not exercised.[4] Stock option and purchase gains in 1958 were scattered, being reported by 11 firms out of the 25 largest.

Despite the reduction in salaries and bonuses, thrift and pension plan benefits continued to gain ground. Income values of pension benefits increased, and thrift benefits were reported by 12 concerns. In the tax picture there was little change visible.

In the foregoing year-by-year review, we looked at changes in individual company types of pay package in a somewhat

4. See Chapter IV, section on contingent credits.

kaleidoscopic fashion. Some of the major developments as they affect the individual company pay package can be viewed in a more accurate and more quantitative way by looking at the history of five representative companies.

Among the 25 companies in the sample for each selected year, 13 companies appeared in every year. The five companies which are shown in Diagram 21 were selected from the 13 as representing distinct variants in the company pay package. The diagram shows for each of the five companies the total pay package before taxes for the three highest paid executives taken together.

The picture for International Harvester includes salary, current bonus, and pension. The emphasis on a currently paid bonus is also typical of Bethlehem Steel. Anaconda Copper had an even simpler pay package for years before 1955, consisting entirely of salary. It is, however, similar in the sense that it emphasized current payments. The International Harvester picture is interesting on two counts: (1) rather atypically the total curve has dropped far below 1929 levels, even if in 1958 it was above the 1942 low; (2) bonuses before World War II constituted a much larger share of the pay package than salaries and fees, but since the war bonuses have been much more modest and smaller than salaries and fees.

The picture for Du Pont shows another typical but distinct type of pay package consisting of salary, bonus, and pension, but this time the bonus is payable over the years following the award instead of currently. This scheme is typical of other companies as well, including the big three in the automobile industry and Gulf Oil. It is apparent that for Du Pont the bonus has provided the great flexible element in the pay package, shrinking from 1929 to 1942, rising until 1956, and then falling again. It also appears that, except in 1937 and 1942, bonuses have comprised a much larger share of the total than have salaries.

The third picture in the diagram is that for Sinclair Oil, and it is significant because it shows a typical oil company pay package—salary, pension, thrift plan benefits, and stock option gains. Among the oil companies in the 25-company sample, most

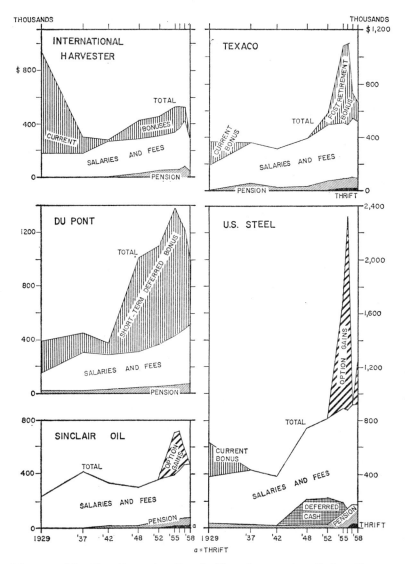

THOUSANDS

INTERNATIONAL HARVESTER

$ 800—

400—

TOTAL

BONUSES

CURRENT

SALARIES AND FEES

0—

PENSION

THOUSANDS

$ 1,200

TEXACO

800

TOTAL

POST-RETIREMENT BONUS

CURRENT BONUS

400

SALARIES AND FEES

PENSION

0

THRIFT

DU PONT

1200—

TOTAL

800—

SHORT-TERM DEFERRED BONUS

400—

SALARIES AND FEES

0—

PENSION

U.S. STEEL

2,400

2,000

1,600

OPTION GAINS

1,200

800

TOTAL

SINCLAIR OIL

800—

TOTAL

400—

OPTION GAINS

SALARIES AND FEES

0—

PENSION

a

CURRENT BONUS

SALARIES AND FEES

400

DEFERRED CASH

PENSION

THRIFT

1929   '37   '42   '48   '52 '55 '58   1929   '37   '42   '48   '52 '55 '58

a = THRIFT

Diagram 21—Top Executive Pay in Five Companies, Before Taxes

131

firms have either this type of pay package or a slight modification of it without stock option gains. For example, the pay package for Standard Oil (California) shows no option gains, while that for Standard of New Jersey does. The Sinclair picture is significant, aside from the general make-up of the pay package, because it shows the increasing diversification of the company's pay package over the years. Before 1937 it was all salary; in 1942 the income value of pensions came into the picture; and from 1955 on, thrift plan benefits and stock option gains showed up as parts of the top executive pay package. Except in 1955 and 1956, salaries were by far the largest element in the total. Stock option gains were a large factor in 1955–1956, but were less important in earlier as well as later years.

The view for Texaco, rather than being typical of oil companies, is just the opposite. Texaco does, however, have a major pay package element, the postretirement bonus, typical of other companies including GE and Gulf Oil, but both the latter have benefits which Texaco does not. The postretirement bonus has added substantially to the pay package for Texaco since 1952, although it has dropped from its peak in 1955–1956. It had a current bonus plan in 1929, but this was abandoned before 1937. Except in 1955 and 1956, salaries and fees have been the largest part of the pay package. Like other oil companies, Texaco has added a thrift plan in recent years.

The last picture in the diagram portrays the before-tax pay package for U.S. Steel. Unlike the other pictures, it is largely a pattern unto itself, although it does reflect many of the changes that were taking place in the top executive pay packages of the largest companies. Like many other companies, U.S. Steel had a current bonus in 1929 that was abandoned by 1937. Along with others, it adopted a stock option plan in the early 1950s, showing particularly sharp gains in 1956, and exhibiting marked ups and downs in the benefits going to top officers. Unlike most non-oil companies in the top 25, U.S. Steel adopted a thrift plan covering its top officers. During the period 1948–1955, the company had in effect contracts providing for fixed deferred cash

132

payments after retirement. These appear to have functioned as a stopgap until pension benefits were increased. Again like many other companies, salaries and fees were the largest single pay element for U.S. Steel, except in one or two years.

For the five companies whose pay packages have been described, management philosophy is reflected in the data. For example, Du Pont management has stressed the idea that a bonus paid largely in stock, by giving the executive a feeling of ownership in the business, ties him more closely to the company's welfare. The desirability of more equal spreading of income through short-term deferment must enter Du Pont's thinking, too. International Harvester has also adhered to bonuses, but there is evidence of shorter range thinking and of a desire to relate reward to effort more closely in time. Texaco's bonus, by contrast, reflects a shift in management thinking away from current income to postretirement receipt of income. Presumably, the holding effect on the executive as well as the tax advantage of postretirement deferment has played a role.

The U.S. Steel pattern reflects early disillusionment with bonuses in a highly cyclical industry. It may also reflect opportunistic thinking, for example, in the use of deferred cash contracts before providing increased pension benefits. For both Sinclair Oil and U.S. Steel, the combination of postretirement deferment and option gains indicates management's seeking more than one approach to tax minimization. The options (including Du Pont more recently) are also evidence of greater management interest in rewarding executive effort by stock appreciation rather than relying on bonus payments which are related more closely to company profits.

Now in addition to comparing the top executive pay package for individual companies on a historical basis, we should also take a cross section view—comparing all 25 companies with each other for a single year—to complete the picture. This is done in Diagrams 22 and 23 for the year 1958. The first shows the 1958 top executive pay package before and after taxes for the three top officers in each company; the second exposes the make-up of that package company by company. In looking at the two diagrams, one should bear in mind that, because we are using a single year, some parts of the pay package may be excluded. For example, certain firms having bonus plans awarded no bonuses in 1958.

From Diagram 22, where the companies are ranked in order of the total pay package before taxes, it is apparent that, with regard to the before-tax situation, Bethlehem Steel ranked ahead of all the other firms by a considerable margin. International Harvester, however, ranked well behind all the others, perhaps reflecting weakness in the agricultural machinery industry. The steel companies exhibited sizeable pay packages by occupying two of the highest positions and a third position well above the middle of the ranking. The automobile manufacturers Ford and GM ranked high on the list, Chrysler near the bottom. Although Gulf Oil and Standard of New Jersey ranked toward the top, most other companies in the oil-refining industry were on lower rungs of the ladder. The two chemical companies were just over the border in the upper half of the ranking. By contrast, the two nonferrous metals companies were in the lower half of the ranking. Performance of the two electrical products manufacturers was split, GE standing close to the top, Westinghouse about in the middle. The one rubber company was also in the middle. Possibly heralding the age of automation, IBM ranked fourth, surpassed only by three other firms.

Industry executives may raise questions as to differences in company ranking before and after taxes, because, although the after-tax ranking generally tends to follow that before taxes, there are obviously a good many exceptions, such as Ford versus Bethlehem Steel. The answers to some of these questions can be considered as we examine Diagram 23.

The composition of the before-tax pay package in 1958 is brought out in Diagram 23, which ranks the different companies according to the percentage of current payment. This follows the simpler method of classification of pay package elements considered earlier in the present chapter—by degree of defer-

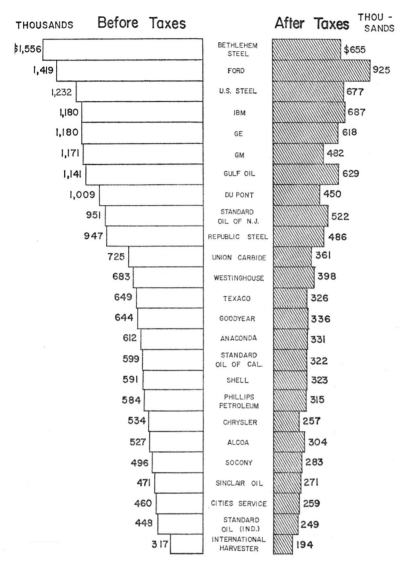

Before Taxes   After Taxes   THOU-
                                                   SANDS

	Before Taxes		After Taxes
$1,556	BETHLEHEM STEEL		$655
1,419	FORD		925
1,232	U.S. STEEL		677
1,180	IBM		687
1,180	GE		618
1,171	GM		482
1,141	GULF OIL		629
1,009	DU PONT		450
951	STANDARD OIL OF N.J.		522
947	REPUBLIC STEEL		486
725	UNION CARBIDE		361
683	WESTINGHOUSE		398
649	TEXACO		326
644	GOODYEAR		336
612	ANACONDA		331
599	STANDARD OIL OF CAL.		322
591	SHELL		323
584	PHILLIPS PETROLEUM		315
534	CHRYSLER		257
527	ALCOA		304
496	SOCONY		283
471	SINCLAIR OIL		271
460	CITIES SERVICE		259
448	STANDARD OIL (IND.)		249
317	INTERNATIONAL HARVESTER		194

Diagram 22—Top Executive Pay in 25 Companies for 1958, Top Three Officers Together

135

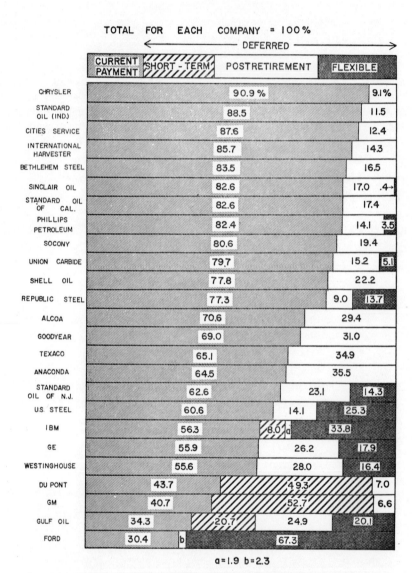

TOTAL FOR EACH COMPANY = 100%

	CURRENT PAYMENT	SHORT-TERM	POSTRETIREMENT	FLEXIBLE
CHRYSLER	90.9%			9.1%
STANDARD OIL (IND.)	88.5			11.5
CITIES SERVICE	87.6			12.4
INTERNATIONAL HARVESTER	85.7			14.3
BETHLEHEM STEEL	83.5			16.5
SINCLAIR OIL	82.6			17.0 .4→
STANDARD OIL OF CAL.	82.6			17.4
PHILLIPS PETROLEUM	82.4			14.1 3.5
SOCONY	80.6			19.4
UNION CARBIDE	79.7			15.2 5.1
SHELL OIL	77.8			22.2
REPUBLIC STEEL	77.3			9.0 13.7
ALCOA	70.6			29.4
GOODYEAR	69.0			31.0
TEXACO	65.1			34.9
ANACONDA	64.5			35.5
STANDARD OIL OF N.J.	62.6		23.1	14.3
U.S. STEEL	60.6		14.1	25.3
IBM	56.3	8.0 a		33.8
GE	55.9		26.2	17.9
WESTINGHOUSE	55.6		28.0	16.4
DU PONT	43.7	49.3		7.0
GM	40.7	52.7		6.6
GULF OIL	34.3	20.7	24.9	20.1
FORD	30.4	b	67.3	

a=1.9 b=2.3

**Diagram 23—The Before-Tax Pay Package in 1958,
25 Companies, Top Three Officers Together**

136

ment. Chrysler, for instance, deferred only about 9 per cent of the before-tax total in postretirement payments, while paying out almost 91 per cent in current income. Other companies included short-term and flexible deferment as well.

By applying this information to Diagram 22, it is possible to explain why, in many cases, the after-tax position of a company differed from its position before taxes. The most noticeable instance was that, although Bethlehem Steel had the largest before-tax total pay package of any of the 25 companies, it was outpaced after taxes by Ford, IBM, and U.S. Steel. The answer to this apparent discrepancy lies in the make-up of the top officers' pay package for each company, and in the taxability of each component. Turning to Diagram 23, one can see that the pay package for Bethlehem Steel was fully taxable either currently or after retirement. By contrast Ford, IBM, and U.S. Steel had flexible deferment income amounting to 67.3 per cent, 33.8 per cent, and 25.3 per cent, respectively, of the pay package. This income, taxable only at capital gains rates, readily accounts not only for the after-tax excess over Bethlehem, but also for the order of companies among the three rival firms.

A comparison of IBM and GE, as seen in Diagram 23, indicates why, of two firms with the same 1958 pretax total, one (IBM) did so much better by its officers after taxes. Again referring to Diagram 23, there was a substantial flexible deferment (stock option) element in both cases. But the IBM figure was 33.8 per cent of the package, while GE had only 17.9 per cent in flexible deferment. This left the IBM top men better off after taxes.

With GM versus Gulf Oil, the question is why GM should be well ahead of Gulf Oil before taxes, and yet run way behind after taxes. The main reason is that Gulf Oil's package included over 20 per cent in the flexible deferment category. Both Gulf and GM had short-term deferred income, which is hit by taxes to about the same extent as current payment. Taking the two items together, GM executives had roughly 93 percent of their income subject to high tax rates, compared to 55 per cent for Gulf. GM had a much smaller share of the top pay package in postretirement deferment —less than 7 per cent, against close to 25 per cent for Gulf—but taxes impinged on it less because it was all in pension income values, while the Gulf Oil postretirement portion included substantial stock allotments. This, but only this factor, favored GM.

The comparison between Du Pont and Standard Oil (New Jersey) is similar to the previous instance, the question involving Du Pont's low after-tax figure compared to Standard of Jersey's. In this case, three factors operated against Du Pont. Standard Oil had 14 per cent of the package in flexible deferment, while Du Pont reported no such gains. Standard had 63 per cent in high-tax current income, while Du Pont had 93 per cent (including current payment and short-term deferred, as in the GM case). Finally, Standard had a higher percentage—23 per cent against 7 per cent—in postretirement deferment. Not only is such income generally subject to lower tax rates, but part of Standard's deferred income consisted of thrift plan benefits taxable only at capital gains rates.

In the case of Union Carbide versus Westinghouse, Union Carbide executives, better off before taxes, did not fare as well afterwards. In this case the postretirement deferment may, if anything, have favored Union Carbide. The proportions—28 per cent for Westinghouse, contrasted to 15 per cent for Union Carbide—appear to be against Union Carbide, but the chemical company's postretirement deferment was all in pension values, while the Westinghouse deferment included a deferred stock bonus involving larger amounts and therefore taxable at slightly higher rates. Any possible advantage to Union Carbide from this factor was more than offset, however, by two big elements favoring Westinghouse. The latter had 16 per cent in flexible deferment against only 5 per cent for Union Carbide. It also had only 56 per cent against Union Carbide's 80 per cent in high-tax current payment.

Comparing Shell and Standard Oil (California), Shell was lagging before taxes, ahead afterwards, in each case by a small margin. These differences are probably not too significant. In

1 3 8

fact the Standard of California total may be somewhat understated, which could easily change the results. On the basis of the estimates used here, however, Shell had a smaller proportion in current payment—78 per cent against 83 per cent for Standard. It also had a correspondingly larger share in postretirement deferment. For both concerns, the postretirement payments were split between pension income values and thrift plan values, with Shell having a larger share in each.

Chrysler, which was ahead of Alcoa before taxes, was behind after taxes. In this instance, the explanation lies entirely in the difference in the share of the total paid currently and the share deferred until after retirement. For Chrysler, the proportions were 91 per cent and 9 per cent, as we have noted. This compared with 71 per cent and 29 per cent for Alcoa. The net result was favorable to the top three executives of Alcoa.

In a comparison of Texaco and Goodyear, the former fared better than the latter before taxes but not as well afterwards. Goodyear had a larger share in current income—69 per cent against 65 per cent for Texaco—and correspondingly less in postretirement deferment. This, of course, would tend to point to just the opposite of the observed result. What accounted for the difference? The key lies in the postretirement stock distribution of bonuses. Both companies have such a plan, but Texaco's was started in early 1950, while the Goodyear bonus, in a form providing deferred contingent compensation for all the top three officers, did not become effective until August, 1952. The result of the lag is that under Texaco's plan substantially larger dollar amounts of stock (future stock valued at 1958 prices) was estimated to be payable upon retirement. This meant tax rates ranging from 58 per cent to 80 per cent on the Texaco stock, but appreciably lower rates, 50 per cent to 70 per cent, on the Goodyear stock. These rates would apply to all shares distributed, including, of course, the 1958 shares. This factor was enough to account for the better showing of Goodyear after taxes.

It is clear from these examples that where the ranking of any pair of firms before taxes differs from the order after taxes, the apparent discrepancy can almost always be explained by inter-company differences in the make-up of the top executive pay package. The reason clearly lies in the varying impact of taxes on the pay elements, a subject which we shall consider at length in the next chapter.

VII

Taxes
and the Total
Pay Package

Tax minimization, as indicated in Chapter VI, is one of the major considerations influencing management in choosing different ways of compensating its top executives. Here we shall explore some of the more important devices used by corporations and individuals to minimize the effect of the federal individual income tax and the capital gains tax on the pay of the top men. We have made no attempt to evaluate the effect of other federal taxes on the executive pay package, because it is not our concern to investigate estate and gift taxes, or to explore the role of personal trusts in relation to top officers (much of this ground has been surveyed in the literature on estate planning). Similarly, no consideration is given to estimates of the impact on top executive pay of state and local taxes.[1] What we shall show is that the effects of

1. It is pertinent to note, however, what the approximate effect of the state income tax is for a large industrial state. For example, the New York State income tax for 1959 on a total income of $100,000, all in salary, works out as follows under the indicated assumptions.

federal taxes not only vary depending on the type of tax, but even differ as to whether their impact is positive or negative. In each case, set against the provisions of the law, the assumptions previously used behind tax computations, and how the devices serve to minimize taxes, we shall indicate the net combined effect of the devices as measured by the percentage of tax against the before-tax figures.

Tax Minimization

An interesting albeit rough measure of the net effect of tax minimization is provided by recent Internal Revenue Service data for a gross adjusted income level of $200 thousand to $500 thousand. At this level, for returns with normal tax and surtax (but no capital gains tax), the effective tax rate against taxable income is 68 per cent. For returns with alternative tax (capital gains tax), this rate would drop to only a little more than 58 per cent. If, however, the tax in the latter case was figured against adjusted gross rather than taxable income, the rate would go down still further to somewhat less than 47 per

1959 New York State Income Tax; Married Couple,
2 Dependents; Total Income $100,000, All Salary:

$100,000	Total income
—15,000	Deductions (at 15 per cent, assuming federal basis of 1957)
$ 85,000	Net income
—2,400	4 exemptions at $600 per exemption
$ 82,600	Taxable balance
—15,000	
$ 67,600	Taxable at 10 per cent
$ 860	Tax on 1st $15,000
6,760	Tax on remainder
$ 7,620	Total
—25	Statutory credit
$ 7,595	Total tax due (or 7.6 per cent of total income)

142

cent.[2] These rates, of course, reflect all income reported, and not merely the corporate segment that is our concern in this study. Nonetheless, the data reveal the wide difference between rates of actual taxes paid and the marginal tax rates written into federal law. The various devices of tax minimization account for the margin, including, for instance, the provision for deductions, the effective tax rate curve, the capital gains provisions, and the dividend credit.

In the preparation of his individual income tax return for the federal government, the executive is allowed to take two quite different types of deductions. The first, which is taken before arriving at adjusted gross income, includes the expense account items already discussed in Chapter V. The other type is deductible from adjusted gross income, and includes such items as certain taxes, contributions, medical expenses, and so forth. It is the second class of deductions which interests us here.

In the earlier examples in this book taxable income was derived in most cases by multiplying adjusted gross income by a percentage deductions rate. In contrast with the unrealistic standard deductions used in some proxy statements[3] the deduction rates used here are historical. They are portrayed in Diagram 24 for the two years 1946 and 1957. The vertical scale in the diagram shows deductions as a per cent of adjusted gross income. The horizontal scale, showing the different levels of adjusted gross income, is semilogarithmic.[4]

For 1944, and all later years, the deductions rates were derived

2. U.S. Treasury Department, *Statistics of Income, Individual Income Tax Returns,* 1957, p. 38, Table 8.

3. See, for example, Bethlehem Steel's proxy statement covering the year 1958, which noted that the after-tax remuneration assumed no other income, two exemptions and a joint return if the executive was married, one return and one exemption for a single officer, and a $1,000 standard deduction.

4. Although such a scale is perhaps unfamilar to some readers, it is necessary when examining income levels over a wide range, in this case from a low of $1,000 to a high of $1,000,000. The longer ticks indicate adjusted gross income levels of $1,000 $10,000 $100,000, and $1,000,000, while the shorter ones represent thousands, tens of thousands, and hundreds of thousands.

as follows. From the appropriate table in *Statistics of Income*,[5] the total of itemized deductions for each adjusted gross income class was divided by the matching adjusted gross income figure. The resulting deductions percentage was plotted at the midpoint of the adjusted gross income class, the final curves making it possible to interpolate for intermediate levels of income.

For 1943 and earlier years, both income classes and amounts of income were reported, not on an adjusted gross income basis, but according to net income. The data used in the study reflect for 1943 and earlier years a technical correction, which has been applied to the original net income data to provide a rough conversion to an adjusted gross income basis. Both the midpoint of each income class and the deductions percentage were recomputed for all years from 1929 through 1943. In general, net income was the income after subtracting deductions from gross income. In the light of this fact, each deductions percentage based on net income was multiplied by the class midpoint to arrive at the amount by which the midpoint would have to be raised to reflect adjusted gross income. Then this amount was divided by the adjusted gross income to get a new deductions percentage.

To give a concrete example, in 1937, the net income class whose midpoint was $125,000 included deductions of $54.9 million against net income of $272.3 million, or a deductions rate on net income of 20.2 per cent. This percentage multiplied by the midpoint gave the amount of the average deduction at the $125,000 net income level, a little over $25,000. Adding the average deduction to the net income midpoint, the sum was a new adjusted gross income class midpoint of $150,000, and dividing the $25,000 deductions by the new midpoint, the quotient was a new deductions percentage on an adjusted gross income basis of 16.7 per cent.

It is fair to conclude from the example that the net effect of recalculating income class midpoints and deductions percentages

5. For example, the latest deductions figures used are for 1957 and were taken from *Statistics of Income 1957, Individual Income Tax Returns,* Table 5, Returns with Itemized Deductions.

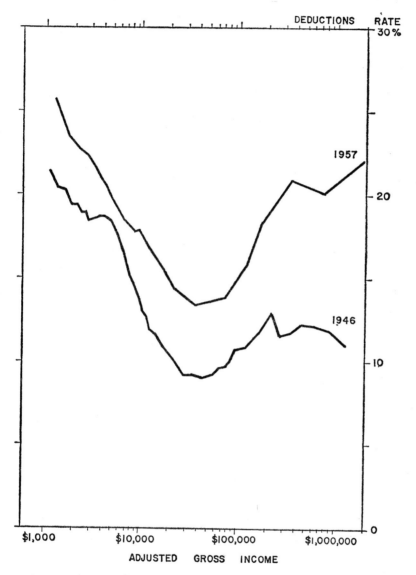

30%

1957

20

1946

10

0

$1,000 $10,000 $100,000 $1,000,000

ADJUSTED   GROSS   INCOME

Diagram 24—Deductions as Per Cent of Adjusted Gross Income

145

to an adjusted gross income basis would be to show higher income levels but lower deductions percentages.

Now deductions can minimize the effective tax rate on the top executive's pay package in two distinct ways. One is through a shift in the prevailing level of rates; the other is by a movement along a given rate curve. For example, using the data in Diagram 24, the tick just to the right of the $100,000 tick is for an income of $200,000. Looking at the line for 1957, it can be seen that the deductions percentage at this income level was around 18 per cent. By contrast, the rate for the same income in 1946 was around 13 per cent. This can be interpreted as follows: if between 1946 and 1957 the schedule of effective tax rates had remained absolutely unchanged, and if an executive had had $200,000 of adjusted gross income in each of the two years, both his taxable income and, because of the lower deductions rate, his tax would show a substantial reduction. This reasoning assumes, of course, that the executive followed the pattern of the average tax return in his income class. This illustrates the effect of a change in the rate schedule.

The other approach can be shown by assuming that for 1957 an executive shifts from a job paying $100,000 to one paying $200,000. His deductions rate, again assuming adherence to the pattern of his income group, would rise from 15 per cent to 18 per cent. The net tax effect of this change is that, although the executive's adjusted gross income would rise, the simultaneous increase in the deductions rate would mean that the effective tax rate would be lower than if the deductions rate stayed the same. In other words, the rise in rate would have a dampening influence on the increase in effective tax.

Effective tax rates are subject to changes, however, which move in the opposite direction from those noted above. For example, a reduction in the whole deductions rate schedule, or a cut in pay of the executive, would work unfavorably for the executive.

Examples in earlier chapters showing tax calculations typically involved the use of an effective tax rate against a level of taxable income. The tax rates used were based on the assumption of a married couple with two dependents. Such an assumption has the disadvantages of understating the tax burden for single men and perhaps of overstating in a few cases the burden for those executives having several dependents. In any case, the assumption has made it possible to use effective rates which are comparable among all executives.

Typical effective tax rate curves are shown in Diagram 25 for the years 1929 and 1954 to date for income levels ranging up to $1,000,000. The vertical scale indicates the tax rate in per cent. The horizontal scale shows taxable income. The scale is semilogarithmic, similar to that used for Diagram 24. The tax curves in Diagram 25 were built by determining the effective rate of tax for selected levels of taxable income, and plotting the curves so that in-between values could be obtained by interpolation. Each taxable income was taken as the income after deductions but before exemptions. Thus the resulting rates reflected not only the tax rate itself, but the allowance for exemptions. Other factors also came into the picture, but these need not be spelled out here (they are made clear in the detailed analysis of the methods used in certain years shown in Appendix III).

The calculations for each year were checked wherever possible against published data on effective tax rates drawn from several sources.[6]

The two rate curves in Diagram 25 provide an interesting contrast. In 1929 the bottom end of the curve showed no tax at all for the lowest income levels, and then a gradual rise. This behavior of the lower end of the tail was characteristic of all the tax rate curves under both Republican and Democratic administrations until about 1939.

After 1939, defense and war demanded increased revenues.

6. *Treasury Bulletin,* February, 1947, Table 1, Part C, pp. A-7 through A-15; Tax Foundation, *Facts and Figures on Government Finance,* various years; *Statistical Abstract of the United States, 1957,* pp. 370–71; U.S. Congress, House, Committee on Ways and Means, *Individual Income Tax Reduction Act of 1953,* 83rd Congress, 1st Session, 1953, H. Rept. 49 to accompany H.R. 1, p. 11.

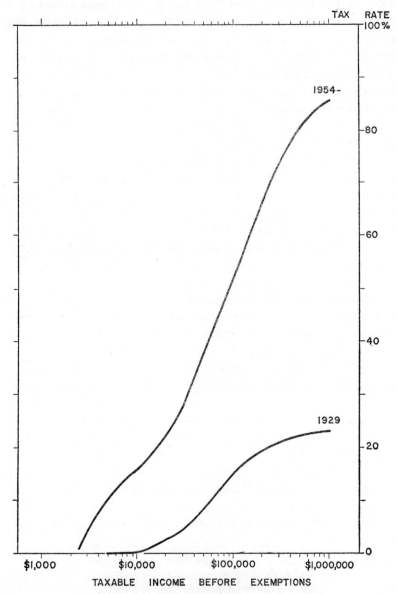

Diagram 25—Individual Income Tax Rates

148

The result was a tendency for the lower tail to bulge, a tendency that has persisted ever since. The reason for the bulge appears to be related to the upper tail of each of the two curves. In 1929 a top rate of 24 per cent left the higher-paid executive with at least three-quarters of his pretax income, even if it was all fully taxable. Having a relatively favorable psychological impact for the executive, this still gave the federal government sufficient revenue without having to create a bulge at the lower end of the curve. By contrast, a top effective rate of 87 per cent, as was true in the curve for 1954 to date, has had only a negative effect on the executive's psychology. The executive passes the 50 per cent effective tax rate level at somewhere around $100,000 of taxable income, but the psychological factor comes into play at a much lower level if we consider the tax on the marginal dollar of income. Because of the rate progression, an executive filing a joint return, allowing for income splitting, must pay at a rate of more than 50 per cent on every dollar of taxable income in excess of $36,000.

That psychology has some effect on revenue collected is realized by tax specialists. It is a well-known fact that the highest levels of income are now far less productive of revenue for the federal government than the lower levels. The number of taxpayers in the highest brackets is so small, despite their large incomes, that not much revenue is involved in the aggregate. By contrast, the number of taxpayers in the lower brackets is so large, despite modest incomes, that enormous amounts of revenue are garnered in total. The result of this is that a substantial change in rates in the highest income levels has about the same effect as, say, the change of a fraction of a percentage point in rates at lower income levels. A former Treasury official has pointed out that "out of over $40 billion of estimated revenue for the current fiscal year, probably not over $800 million, or less than 2% comes from the rates over 50%."[7]

The tax rate curves as shown in Diagram 25 can be used to an extent—more limited than is sometimes thought—for tax mini-

7. See Dan T. Smith, "New Ideas for a 'Revolution' in Taxes," *U.S. News and World Report,* January 18, 1960, p. 67.

149

mization. Over the longer run, management can make adjustments in pay arrangements that rely on a change in the entire level of rates. It may be that an important part of the thinking as to postretirement payments relates to the expectation (or hope) of lower tax rate schedules at some time in the future. The higher rate schedules of more recent years have made even more important the idea of minimization by tapping a lower level of taxable income on the curve, thus subjecting income to a lower rate of tax.

This strategy may be illustrated by the GM plan, which provides for short-term deferment of bonus payments. It is sometimes supposed that this plan results in enormous tax savings, often based on the idea that a single large bonus spread over several years will result in a lower taxable income for each year. This, however, has been true only in part. It was true in the years immediately after World War II, when there was less overlapping of income. It has also been true to the extent that awards overlap into retirement, when income layers are built over a pension rather than on top of the higher salary base. But the evidence of this study is that, where the awards are payable on top of a salary (and even without allowing for appreciation of the stock for years after 1958), the overlapping of layers of income from year after year of bonuses has wiped out the tax advantage of short-term deferment.

With postretirement deferment, on the other hand, there appears to be an enormous difference in the effectiveness of pensions and deferred cash payments under contract on one side, and postretirement deferred stock bonuses such as those under the GE plan on the other. Pension payments in World War II suddenly increased in popularity when wages and salaries were frozen, and where extra incentives were sought to attract executives (and others as well). Long after wage and salary controls were removed, pensions remained popular and benefits were increased. One reason for this was that an increase in pension was worth more to the executive than the corresponding amount in salary. Pension consultants have often argued for a level of pension which would be approximately 50 per cent of an executive's final pay at retirement. Tax rate schedules remaining the same, this would mean that upon retirement, the executive's income could be expected to touch a much lower income level on the effective tax rate curve. Thus, both pensions and deferred cash payments under contract take maximum advantage of the tax-minimizing strategy of movement along the effective tax rate curve.[8]

The foregoing is less marked, however, if other income such as a postretirement bonus, especially in stock, is paid out along with a pension. For example, under the GE plan, the piling up of shares of stock under repeated bonus awards and the accumulation of both pre- and postretirement dividends tend to boost postretirement income up to a level at which the tax-minimizing effect of touching a lower point on the rate curve is substantially offset.

Another method of tax minimization is through the capital gains tax rates (26 per cent for 1952 and 1953 and 25 per cent for all other years since 1942). Their use has been noted with regard to thrift plan benefits, and also in connection with both stock option and purchase gains, although these apply almost entirely to 1952 and later years.

Under the tax regulations in effect since the passage of the Revenue Act of 1942, the special long-term capital gains rates apply only to assets held more than six months. Long-term capital gains are included in income only to the extent of half the gain, and under present regulations this half is taxed either at the full rate or at a 50 per cent rate (in the latter case, making 25 per cent the effective rate on capital gains). Whether full rates or capital gains rates apply depends on which results in the lesser tax.

The particular point at which the alternative tax comes into effect varies, depending on factors such as the type of return, the amount of the net long-term capital gain, and the prevailing tax rates for fully taxable and capital gains income. These points can

8. See Appendix IV for assumptions concerning taxable income from pensions.

be brought out in examples by assuming a joint return and seeing what happens when the amount of the capital gain or the tax rate structure is changed.

Under the tax rates in effect from 1954 on, if a net long-term capital gain of $10,000 is assumed, the break-even point, after which the alternative tax applies, is reached at a level of taxable income after exemptions of $36,500. But if the capital gains portion of the income is assumed instead to be $20,000, the break-even point rises to $39,000. This is what may happen when the amount of the capital gain is changed.

To see what the situation is with a change in the tax rate structure, suppose that the gain is as cited above, $10,000 of long-term capital gains, but that instead of the 1954 rate structure, the much lower rate structure (when the tax credits then in the law are allowed for) of 1948 is assumed. The result is to change the break-even point from $36,500 to the vicinity of $45,400.

Although there is some variation in the break-even point, as noted in the examples, tax specialists nevertheless make it a practice to check for possible application of the alternative tax, for a joint return, if taxable income is $36,000 or more.[9]

The importance of the break-even mechanism provided in the law, insofar as this study is concerned, has to do with stock option and purchase gains and with benefits arising under thrift plans. A glance at the option figures reveals that they are tied in with current compensation, which typically runs at levels far above the break-even points mentioned. Thrift plan benefits are in a different category, since actual payment typically falls in the first year of the much lower levels of retirement income. For this reason, the retirement income of almost 60 executives, who have received or will receive thrift benefits, was checked to ascertain whether under the regulations the alternative tax would come into effect, resulting in the application of capital gains rates. Most of the officers were checked by comparing total taxable income in the first year of retirement with the break-even points indicated in the

9. Commerce Clearing House, *Federal Tax Course 1958,* par. 1717, p. 1924.

earlier examples. For about 10 companies, it was necessary to use the total of the first year's retirement income including a rough estimate of the capital gain derived from the payment of thrift benefits. In only one instance do the results clearly indicate that capital gains rates would not apply.

The tax-minimizing effect of capital gains treatment of stock option and purchase gains, and of thrift plan benefits with long-term capital gains rates of 25 or 26 per cent, needs little elaboration in the light of the obviously sizeable difference between these rates and those paid by the top officer on fully taxable income, as evidenced in Diagram 25. In the struggle by corporations and their tax experts to minimize taxes on executive pay, this device appears to be the most effective of all.

The fourth principal device for minimizing taxes for top executives is the dividend credit. Under various stock bonus plans, and under Du Pont's dividend unit scheme mentioned in Chapter IV, the amount of tax was reduced in each case by 4 per cent of dividends for 1954 and later years, because of the provision for a tax credit on dividends contained in the 1954 Code. The provision is more complicated than the mere application of the tax credit per se. In the first place, the law allows on a joint return for the exclusion from income of up to $100 of dividends. The 4 per cent credit is then based on the remaining dividends. The law further provides that the credit may be no more than 4 per cent of taxable income, nor more than the amount of the income tax reduced by the foreign tax credit.[10]

In order for the first of the two restrictions on the amount of the credit to become effective, the top executive's taxable income would have to be less than the nonexcluded portion of dividend income. Even with generous deductions, this would appear to be most atypical. For the second limitation to apply would seem even more unlikely. The rates of tax which bear on top officers preclude this possibility. Thus, only a simple application of the 4 per cent credit is warranted in our study.

10. Commerce Clearing House, *Federal Tax Course 1958,* par. 210, spells out these provisions in detail.

153

In regard to the tax-minimizing effect of the dividend credit, it would appear that this is probably more important in connection with the top executive's income as an investor than it is with respect to his role as a corporate officer, with which we are primarily concerned. But the various plans which provide for deferred stock bonuses do, of course, take advantage of this provision. Perhaps a more obvious indication of its importance is the dividend unit scheme put into effect by Du Pont.

Trends in the Tax Impact on Top Executive Pay

Having considered the various devices used by management in minimizing the taxes on the top executive's pay package, we may now turn to what the results of these activities have been. In the interpretation of diagrams to follow, however, one particular thought should be kept in mind. The tax percentages shown are not the same as those in Diagram 25. In the earlier diagram, tax rates were the rates of tax for given levels of taxable income before exemptions. The rates shown in the new diagrams are simply the difference between the before- and after-tax amounts divided by the before-tax amount. They therefore reflect, not only the tax rate against taxable income, but other factors such as the deductions rate applying to the adjusted gross income, and the actual level of income itself. Often a changing percentage of tax did not mean any change in tax rates at all, but merely a movement up or down along a given rate curve.

What has happened to the effective tax rate on the total 25-company pay package over the years from 1929 to 1958 is shown in Diagram 26. The solid line represents the tax on the total pay package for the three highest paid officers; the dashed line shows the rate applying to current payment; and the gap between the two can be taken as a rough measure of management's success in

154

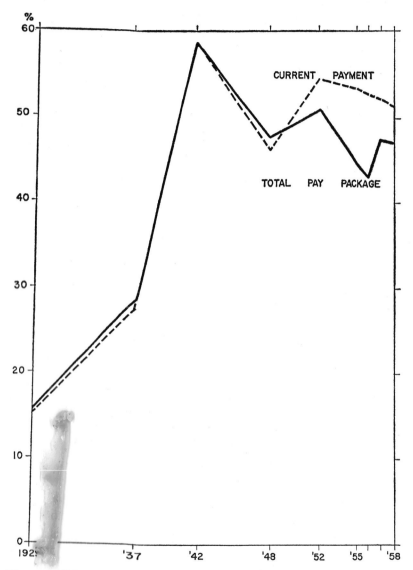

Diagram 26—Tax on Current Payment and on Total Pay Package,
Averages for Top Three Officers

155

developing forms of executive compensation which minimize the high tax rates that go with current payment.[11]

The diagram clearly shows that the tax rate on the total pay package followed the rising income tax curves to reach a wartime high in 1942, fell in 1948 after World War II, rose in 1952 with war in Korea, and despite fluctuation remained high thereafter. Before 1952 (insofar as can be seen from the years sampled), management had relatively little success in avoiding the full impact of progressive individual income tax rates, but since then it has scored decidedly, as evidenced by the wider gap between the two lines. This was especially marked in 1955 and 1956. The cause of the gap has been the increase in the flexible deferment portion of the pay package—stock option and purchase gains. Such gains were pronounced in the two years cited, when the gap was the widest. One curious point brought out by the diagram is that, in some years, the rate on the total pay package was actually higher than that on income paid currently. The reason for this will become apparent from our analysis of Diagram 27.

The effective tax rate on major elements in the total pay package is traced in Diagram 27. The solid and dashed lines at the top, representing short-term deferment and current payment, tend to follow the historical movement of tax rates. The next solid line, for postretirement deferment, is cast in a different mold, although the income is still for the most part fully taxable. The line at the bottom, which represents flexible deferment, although earlier in the fully taxable class, has, since 1948, closely reflected the capital gains rates.

The chief lesson of the diagram is that, for the 25-company sample, top executive pay in the form of short-term deferment has

11. A more precise measure would be to compute what the deductions and taxes would be for each executive, assuming that the whole pay package was paid currently, and then to get the tax rate as a per cent of the total pay package before taxes. This percentage could be compared more accurately with the tax on the total pay package as shown in Diagram 26. However, it is doubtful that the more elaborate computations would yield greatly different results.

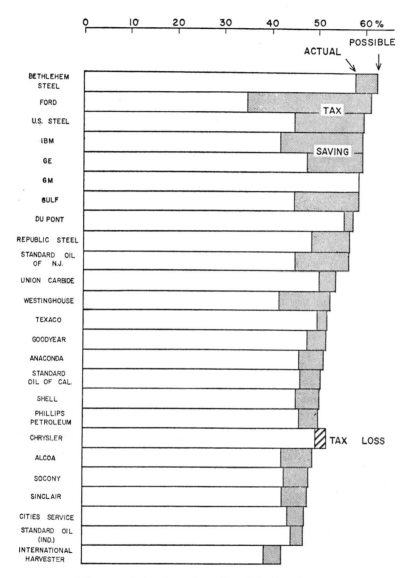

**Diagram 28—Actual vs. Possible Tax Rates,
Averages for Top Three Officers in 1958**

the entire before-tax pay package of each of the three executives in the company were subject to full individual income tax rates. The tax rates reflect deductions computed in the usual way. These rates are the possible percentages. Also shown are actual rates. It will be remembered that in Chapter VI figures were shown, taking the three top officers together, for the total pay package both before and after taxes, for each of the 25 largest companies. These data are the basis for the actual rates.[13]

The shaded portion of each bar shows the "savings," or the extent to which the actual percentage differed from the possible percentage which would result from fully progressive rates applying to the total pay package. The single black-and-white striped patch for Chrysler represents a loss. In that instance the total bar is the actual rate, while the part of the bar out to where the stripes begin represents the possible percentage.

One can see from the diagram that the greatest savings were made by Ford, whose actual tax stood in 1958 at roughly 35 per cent, while the possible tax was 61 per cent. The 35 per cent tax rate actually paid by Ford's top three ($473,000 average before taxes) is the equivalent of the rate for, say, a $66,000 executive whose income was fully taxable. It should be noted that all companies in which the saving between the actual and possible was 10 percentage points or more, had option gains in the pay packages of their top officers. Chrysler, which suffered a tax loss, GM, which just broke even, and Du Pont, which saved little, all provide their executives with short-term deferred bonuses.

Referring only to the actual data, figures for other years would undoubtedly show a somewhat different order of companies, especially depending on when options were exercised. Nonetheless, the general order would tend to be about the same for recent years. The reasons for this again lie in the composition of the pay package, discussed earlier in Chapter VI.

13. Actual rates as used here are based on estimates of the tax on that portion of an executive's pay which comes to him in his capacity as a corporate officer.

Taxes and Equity

Devices used by management to minimize the impact of taxes on the top executive's pay package are often attacked as being inequitable or discriminatory. This type of charge has recently been aimed against stock options in particular. Stock options are often charged with being discriminatory, because they typically are granted to a handful of people at the top of the corporate ladder. For example, the dean of the Harvard Law School has this to say: "Stock options are inherently discriminatory. They can be limited to one employee or a few employees, and ordinarily are. They can be granted in very large amounts, without any of the mild safeguards against discrimination which are provided in the case of pension plans."[14]

The pension safeguards to which he alluded include, for example, a stipulation that whereas qualification may be determined by the employer, it must be found by the Commissioner of Internal Revenue "not to be discriminatory in favor of employees who are officers, shareholders, supervisory employees, or highly paid employees."[15] That such discrimination is clearly present in stock option plans, there can be no reasonable doubt. But the matter does not stop here. It also applies to a large number of other pay plans which are nonqualified on the basis of Treasury Department standards. For instance, stock bonus plans often fall into this category. In fact, many of the extra compensation plans among the 25 largest manufacturing companies fall into the nonqualified classification. That is, they are discriminatory in the sense quoted above.

There are two reasons why this is true. One is that the cost of

14. U.S. House, Committee on Ways and Means, statement by Erwin N. Griswold, December 7, 1959, quoted in U.S. SEC, Division of Corporate Regulation, *Proposed Findings and Conclusions of the Division of Corporate Regulation in the Matter of Middle South Utilities, Inc.*, File No. 70–3777, Appendix F.

15. Commerce Clearing House, Inc., *Federal Tax Course 1958*, par. 2603, p. 2806.

extending these plans to all employees would be so great as to result in their abandonment in many cases. The other reason is that all such plans have a common aim: to offset, or minimize, in one way or another, what is generally regarded by top executives as discrimination against them in the form of excessively high rates of the federal individual income tax. Thus discrimination can be argued two ways.

VIII

Differentials
Among the Top Three

We saw in the previous chapter something of the effects of taxes on the pay package for the top three executives in each company, considered as a group. Of course taxes also affect pay differentials among the top three.[1] Taxes tend to narrow these differentials, while management policy tends on the other hand to widen them.

The question of differentials may be thought of in terms of an economic ladder. For most of us, it is easy enough to climb on

1. Differentials viewed in such a narrow focus may appear to be an esoteric subject, but this need not be so if differentials among the upper rungs of the ladder give an indication of what is happening throughout the organization. E. C. Bursk writing in "Thinking Ahead," *Harvard Business Review,* XXX, No. 2 (March–April, 1952), pp. 141–156, made a study of 41 companies in an attempt to compare the relative progress of different groups of employees within the corporate structure for the two spot years 1939 and 1950. Adjustments were made to reflect taxes and changes in the cost of living. Corporate employees were broken down into the following groups: (1) top management or the top .1 per cent of employees; (2) middle management, taken as the next .9 per cent of

the bottom rung, but as one tries to go up the ladder it becomes shakier and the risk of falling seems greater. In the case of the economic ladder, as the going becomes more difficult, the rewards become greater—more money and other benefits for those who can climb up to the next rung. A person's viewpoint about the ladder, the obstacles to the climb, the extra effort which may be called for, and the size and nature of the reward, all depend to a large extent on his position on the ladder.

In considering the question in this study for the top three rungs of the ladder, we shall first consider possible standards as to the appropriate size of the differential. Then, after examining the problems inherent in measuring differentials among the top three, we shall explore the trends indicated when the various measures are applied to the 25-company sample. We shall also consider the future outlook for differentials.

Standards as to Differentials

There does not appear to be any clear-cut agreement as to how differentials should be set between different ranks in the management hierarchy. However, there would presumably be agreement that dollar margins between organizational levels cannot be the same for the $100,000 executive as they are for the $10,000 executive. Some account has to be taken of the level of pay.

An articulate spokesman on this subject has been Crawford Greenewalt, president of Du Pont. He has put the case this way:

employees; (3) all other supervisory personnel; and (4) hourly paid workers and nonsupervisory white collar employees.

One of the important conclusions of the survey was that the bottom group was relatively better off than it had been and the other groups relatively worse off. Since the cost of living effect was presumably applied in similar fashion to all groups, it would appear that the results clearly implied a narrowing of differentials, among the groups measured, over the 1939–1950 period. The results cited in this article are consistent with the findings of the present study. However, the two spot years 1939 and 1950 do not reflect the effect of stock option gains, which, since 1950, have completely altered the top executive pay package for many of the largest companies.

If compensation is to provide incentive, the scale must be calibrated from the bottom up rather than from the top level down, with a sufficient differential between one level and the next to make promotion attractive. There are many rungs in the corporate ladder of responsibility. In the Du Pont Company, we recognize sixteen positional levels between wage earner and president. Compensation at each of these levels must be sufficiently greater to tempt the man below to make the climb. . . . For the progression to be meaningful, it must be on an after-tax basis. If we say an increase of 25% after taxes for each rung of the ladder is reasonable, simple arithmetic pushes gross compensation at the top into stratospheric levels which do little more than arouse employee and stockholder indignation and make the incumbent wonder whether a take-home pay of 9 cents on the dollar is worth all the censure and abuse.[2]

Asked from the floor what the company did about this, Greenewalt stated, "We take the censure and abuse!" Not all management observers, however, would argue that percentage differentials have to be kept at some arbitrary level after taxes. For example, George G. Hyde, a consulting engineer, has offered, as an illustrative example for a factory organization, a percentage differential, apparently before taxes, of roughly 21 per cent between levels.[3]

Both on practical and theoretical grounds an argument can be made for percentage differentials, either before or after taxes, which are different at various levels of pay. The practical argument would be that constant percentage differentials may result in a corporation's losing personnel, when market supply and demand for a key job have set a price higher than that resulting from the company's internal pay structure. The theoretical case might rest on the idea that while differentials should be computed in relation to pay, the percentage can range either from low to high, or even in reverse from high to low, as one goes up the pay scale. Depending on the actual percentages, the resulting dollar margins might still provide sufficient incentive.

2. Crawford H. Greenewalt, "Incentives and Rewards," Second of 1958 McKinsey Foundation Lectures, delivered at the Graduate School of Business, Columbia University on April 22, 1958, pp. 11–12 of mimeographed release.

3. George G. Hyde, *Fundamentals of Successful Manufacturing* (New York and London: McGraw-Hill, 1946), p. 134.

Measuring Differentials

Measuring the differentials among the top three executives in terms of the total pay package is a more complex proposition than if salaries only were used as the guide. But the added complexity is merited by the greater significance of a measure which reflects major fringe benefits. To select the three highest paid officers,[4] as pointed out in Chapter I, "aggregate remuneration," or salaries where the former was not shown, was the basis used. The records were also examined, however, to see if other pay elements such as pension benefits, stock options, and so on might have a material effect on determining who the top three were. Where this was the case, more than three officers were recorded, with the thought that the decision as to who really were the top three could be made later.

In a fair number of instances extra executives were tentatively included where more than one officer received the same level of pay. These problem cases were resolved later in two different ways. Where one of two executives, otherwise equally paid, received or would receive no postretirement benefits because of early death, the living executive was included as being the more representative. In many more instances, however, the determination was made on the basis of which executive had greater continuity of service.

In some cases company reports to the SEC included only three executives, almost always on the basis of "Aggregate Remuneration." This was particularly true for smaller companies in the sample and in the earlier years. Where this was so, the three officers reported had to be treated as being the three highest paid for the purposes of this study.

As a result of the calculating process, the remaining doubtful cases were decided. Most frequently but not always, this called for a determination of who was the third highest paid officer. In

4. Such factors as a shift taking place in the top management of a firm in a particular year were found to cause trends of differentials for individual companies to be erratic. Using the grouped data avoided this difficulty.

most cases the determination hinged on the exercise of an option or on the calculation of the income value of future pension payments. The example of Republic Steel's top three in 1955 is illustrative of the situation. The three top men, based on salaries and fees as shown in the proxy statement, received respectively $310,000, $250,000 and $171,000. The income values of the pensions for the three did not differ enough to affect the order of executives. But a consideration of the option gains of the three resulted in reversing the order of the first two executives, since the supposedly second highest had option gains of $547,000 compared to $178,000 for the supposedly highest paid man. The third man also had options, but since they were smaller in amount, his position was not affected.

This brings up a puzzling question that was raised by an analysis of differentials based on the total pay package: should differentials be considered according to the order of executives based on the total pay package or on the total pay package less option gains? Without a detailed analysis, one might suppose that it would not make too much difference, since the highest paid executive might be expected to show the largest option gains, the next highest paid executive the next largest gains, and the third highest the smallest gains. However, a company-by-company examination of actual cases showed that, far from uniformly reinforcing the margins which would otherwise have existed, option gains have been haphazard in effect, sometimes working in just the opposite direction and sometimes even eliminating margins altogether.

The data in the Republic Steel example can be further analyzed to illustrate this phenomenon. The high-option executive, with $810,000 of total pay, had a margin of $295,000 over the next man. But for the pay package excluding option gains, he had a negative margin of $74,000, offset by a positive margin of $369,-000 on the option gains. The negative margin is a more significant one because it is intended, as is evidenced by the salary totals cited earlier. Moreover, it reflects the normal organizational relationship within the company. The option gain is windfall, and an order of executives, with rank determined by windfall effect reflected in the total pay package, is unrealistic. This reasoning is bolstered by the fact that, if we had looked at option shares granted rather than exercised, there would have been no reversal of order due to stock options.

For the reasons just indicated, an extensive technical correction of all the option and total pay package data for each of the three highest executives was made. This was done in such a way that the order of executives would be based, not on the total pay package, but on the total pay package excluding options.[5] The general effect of the technical correction on the data for each of the three highest paid executives over the period 1929–1958 can be seen in Diagram 29.

From the diagram, it is easy to see that, for the highest paid executive, the effect of the technical correction was to reduce the amounts shown; whereas, for the third highest paid, the effect of the correction was to increase the amounts shown. In the case of the second highest paid officer, the effect of the correction was to reduce the amounts shown each year except for 1956, when the reverse took place. It is also clear that changes in the totals for each executive had a visible effect on the dollar and percentage differentials that otherwise would have resulted.

Trends of Differentials
Among the Top Three

We are now ready to consider what the measures of differentials show when they are applied to the 25-company sample over the period 1929–1958. In the diagrams that follow, only the order

5. For the most part the technical correction resulted in changes between the second and third highest paid executives. However, no attempt was made to reconsider each executive who had earlier been discarded as a result of the computing process, nor was any attempt made to re-examine the original records, most of which are in Washington. While the technical correction is not completely adequate, it is believed that the degree of inaccuracy in the figures would not change any of the major findings of this study with respect to differentials.

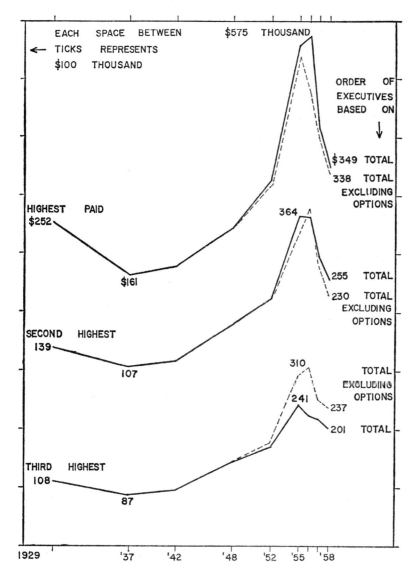

EACH SPACE BETWEEN
← TICKS REPRESENTS
$100 THOUSAND

$575 THOUSAND

ORDER OF
EXECUTIVES
BASED ON
↓

$349 TOTAL
338 TOTAL
EXCLUDING
OPTIONS

HIGHEST PAID
$252

$161

364 ∧

255 TOTAL
230 TOTAL
EXCLUDING
OPTIONS

SECOND HIGHEST
139

107

310 TOTAL
EXCLUDING
OPTIONS

241 237

201 TOTAL

THIRD HIGHEST
108

87

1929   '37   '42   '48   '52   '55   '58

Diagram 29—Average Pay Before Taxes, Alternative Methods

169

of executives based on the total pay package excluding options is used.

First, in Diagram 30, an over-all view showing trends in average pay for each of the three highest paid executives is presented. One advantage of looking at the actual curves is that the relationship between the movement of curves and the dollar differences is brought out.

From the diagram we can see that the average pay of each of the three top officers before taxes fell from 1929 to 1937, rose to a peak in 1955 or 1956, and fell again, but in each instance to a point higher than that of 1929. Throughout the 1929–1958 period the highest paid executive, before taxes, held a greater lead over the second highest officer than did the second over the third. Finally, we may conclude that instead of dollar differentials being reduced—at least before taxes—during a period of rising pay, they tend to widen as pay increases. Conversely, they tend to narrow when the averages decline.

Dollar differentials, observed in the rough in Diagram 30, are shown in closer focus in Diagrams 31 and 32. Both the latter show the average dollar differentials each year for the highest paid over the second highest, and for the second highest over the third. In each diagram, a dashed line has been added to show what the differentials would be if stock option and purchase gains were excluded from the pay package. Diagram 1 shows the situation before taxes and Diagram 32 the picture after taxes.

From the two diagrams we can summarize that before taxes the dollar differential between the average pay for the highest paid executive and that for the second highest dropped from more than $113,000 in 1929, to less than $54,000 in 1937. After that it rose, at first slowly, then skyrocketed to $205,000; thereafter it dropped and vacillated around a level not too different from that of 1929. If options are excluded from the averages, the upward recovery was smaller, having reached in 1958 a level of around $90,000, which is below the 1929 level but well above that of 1937. Furthermore, the trend was less volatile.

The dollar margin paid for the second highest over the third

1 7 0

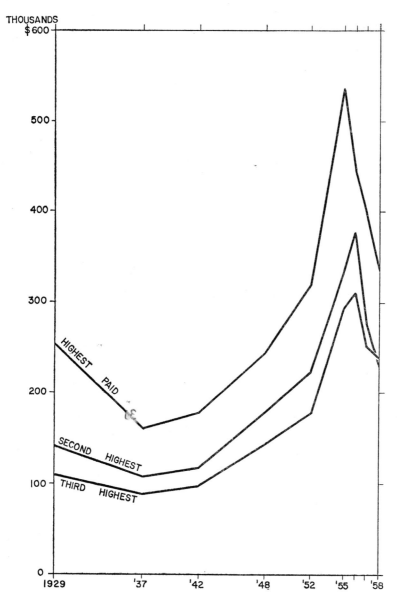

THOUSANDS
$ 600

500

400

300

HIGHEST PAID

200

SECOND HIGHEST

100

THIRD HIGHEST

0

1929   '37   '42   '48   '52   '55   '58

Diagram 30—Average Pay Per Executive Before Taxes

171

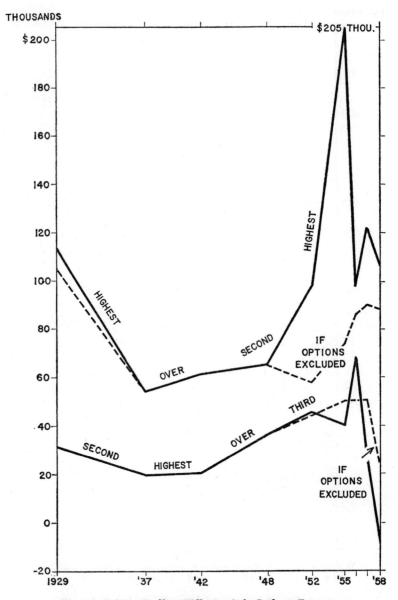

THOUSANDS

$205 THOU.

HIGHEST

HIGHEST

OVER

SECOND

IF
OPTIONS
EXCLUDED

SECOND

HIGHEST

OVER

THIRD

IF
OPTIONS
EXCLUDED

1929   '37   '42   '48   '52   '55   '58

Diagram 31—Dollar Differentials Before Taxes

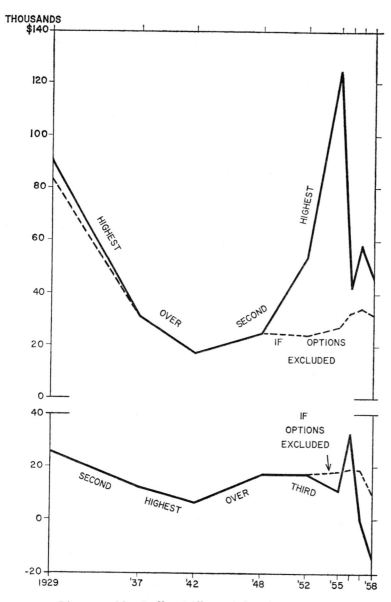

Diagram 32—Dollar Differentials After Taxes

173

fell only moderately from 1929 to 1937, climbed until 1952, fluctuated somewhat, and finally dropped into oblivion, registering a minus $7,000 in 1958 before taxes. Excluding options, the second man's margin rose from 1952 until 1957, and then fell back to just slightly above the 1937 and 1942 levels. The sharper drop in the more inclusive curve resulted from more extensive exercise of options in 1957 and 1958 by the third- than by the second-ranking officer.

After taxes, the shapes of the curves are similar to those before, but the declines continued to 1942 before the trends were reversed. While the margin of the highest paid executive showed a recovery, the net movement ended far below the 1929 level. The margin of the second highest paid man over the third, however, was a negative one of $14,000 by 1958.

For the top officer, the after-tax gain which took place was aided greatly by option gains, but there was a real gain even without the options over the 1942 low. For the second highest paid, excluding the effect of the options, an upward trend from 1942 is evident, although in 1958 the margin was below that for 1937.

The third way in which we shall analyze trends is in terms of percentage differentials. These are pictured in Diagrams 33 and 34, both before and after taxes, as well as including and excluding stock option gains. The percentage differentials are based on the pay averages for each of the three highest paid officers.

The two diagrams indicate that, when stated in percentages, the fall-followed-by-a-rise picture evident for dollar margins is displaced by pronounced, though interrupted, declines. This is true both before and after taxes. Before taxes, the percentage margin for the highest paid over the second highest took a downward trip resembling a toboggan run at St. Moritz. It fell from 82 per cent in 1929 to around 50 per cent in 1937, rose slightly in 1942, and fell again to about 37 per cent in 1948. It has since ridden up and down, being in 1958 a little over 45 per cent, which is higher than the lows in 1948 and 1956.

The per cent margin of the second highest over the third

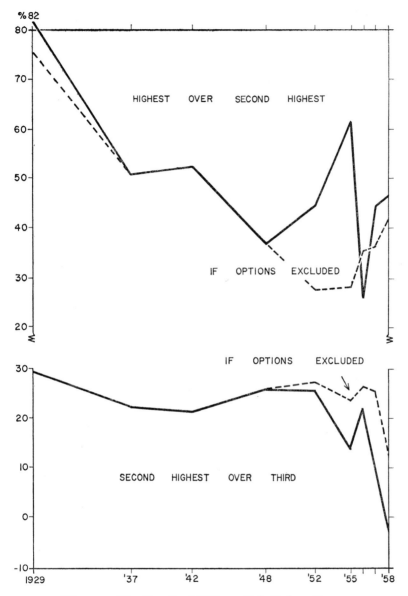

Diagram 33—Per Cent Differentials Before Taxes

175

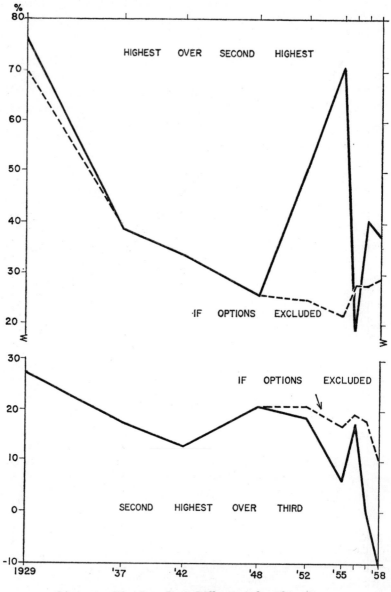

Diagram 34—Per Cent Differentials After Taxes

176

dropped, before taxes, from around 30 per cent in 1929 down to 21 per cent in 1942. There was a temporary rise from 1942 to 1948, followed by a bumpy downhill run ending in a minus 3 per cent for 1958. In short, the differential was wiped out.

Although part of the recovery in the top man's percentage margin is traceable to option gains, by no means all of it is. Contrastingly, for the second highest paid executive's margin, options had a reverse effect, accounting for much, but again not all, of the decline in the last few years.

After taxes, the margin of the highest paid officer follows a curve similar to that before taxes. But it ends in 1958 at around 38 per cent, compared to 46 per cent before taxes. The margin of the second highest over the third, which before taxes dropped to minus 3 per cent, after taxes registered a minus 10 per cent.

As was the case before taxes, options accounted for most of the recovery of the top man's margin after taxes, and for the collapse of the second officer's margin. With the exclusion of options, the differential of the highest paid executive in 1958 was around 29 per cent, but that for the second highest officer was only about 10 per cent.

Possible Future Widening of Differentials

For the purpose of obtaining the total pay package, we included stock option benefits on the basis of exercise, which reflected receipt of the capital gain, even if unrealized. Although this resulted in a gain, say, over 1948, in the percentage differential before taxes of the highest paid executive, that for the second highest man disappeared altogether (see Diagram 33). Nevertheless, it may be that the latter circumstance is temporary, the result of the difference between exercise as opposed to grant of options.

An examination of proxies shows that shares granted under

options, while varying from year to year, still tend to be in proportion to each executive's direct compensation. Thus the executive who is otherwise higher paid is likely to be granted a proportionately larger number of shares under option. It follows that, despite year-to-year changes, the longer-run result will be for the exercise of options to give relatively larger capital gains to the highest paid compared to the second highest, and to the second highest compared to the third. And this would also apply to executives receiving options as a group compared to other groups in the corporation.

If options are excluded, however, after-tax percentage differentials for the first and second highest paid executives were respectively 29 per cent and 10 per cent in 1958 (see Diagram 34). For the highest paid the figure was a little above 1948. For the second highest, it was down from something over 20 per cent in that year; but perhaps most of the drop can be blamed on the 1958 recession, since in 1957 the figure was 18 per cent.

Putting all these facts together, it would seem that over a longer period of years, other conditions being equal, the greater option gains added to the trend of other pay elements may well mean a new tendency toward a broadening of differentials among the top three, and for those employees benefiting from stock options compared to other groups within a corporation.

Although many other factors, such as business conditions, war and peace, and the moral climate of the times, all play a part in determining which of the two possible trends will prevail—a continuation of the past resulting in narrowing of differentials, or a reversal resulting in their widening—it would appear that much will depend on future legislative and tax treatment of stock options and other types of executive compensation. Either removal of the special tax treatment of the restricted stock option, or higher levels of personal income taxes would tend to force after-tax percentage differentials downward. On the other hand, maintenance of the special tax treatment of options and continuation of present rates of federal income taxes could result, over a period of time, in the widening of percentage differentials even after taxes.

178

IX

The Significance
of the Trends

In our study we developed new techniques for measuring the top executive pay package, including not only direct payments, but major fringe benefits as well. Now we can consider the significance of our findings and how some of the trends discovered are likely to move in the future. We shall review them in terms of their influence on various aspects of executive pay and performance; we shall take a look at them in relation to government regulatory and tax policies; and we shall regard them in the light of questions of equity concerning the distribution of income among different occupations in our society.

Various Aspects
of Executive Pay and Performance

There appears to be an inclination among some people to refer to the market for top executive ability in terms of supply and demand, just as if one were speaking of any other product or service. Not all analysts of the subject would agree with that. For example, Roberts talks of a weakening of the concept of a "market for executives."[1] He states that the amount of job shifting by executives is limited, and that most shifts are made by a small fraction of executives who change jobs frequently.[2] He goes on to assert "that the absolute dollar level of a firm's compensation and its relationship to the levels of other companies do not affect incentive."[3] Instead, he lays stress on internal company factors such as the number of layers within the organization as having a much greater influence on executive pay.

A contrast to these views is provided by Sanders, who stresses the role of competition with respect to top executives' pay:

Competition for the consumer's dollar exerts the same downward pressure on executive compensation as on other business costs. Competition for the corporation's dollar, especially between executives and the labor unions, but also to a smaller extent between stockholders and employees generally, operates in the same direction. Competition among corporations for the limited supply of executive ability tends in the opposite direction; it joins with tax increases in serving to push executive compensation up.[4]

Evidence of two different kinds, which bears on the validity of the two contrasting views cited here, has been developed in our study. One type of evidence relates to the personal histories of the top executives. The typical top executive started with one of the 25 largest companies between the ages of twenty-one and twenty-five; and for those who have already retired, typical retirement was in the sixty-one to sixty-five age group. An analysis of 176 top executives who retired in the 1929–1958 period reveals that the typical executive left the company after 36 years of service. An analysis was made of the 32 top executives, included in the 176, who had less than 25 years of service. This revealed that only three left to join a competitor company. Out

1. Roberts, *op. cit.,* p. 100.
2. *Ibid.,* p. 109.
3. *Ibid.,* p. 160.
4. Sanders, *op. cit.,* p. 107.

of the 32 men, 12 had been with a competitor company before joining one of the largest firms, while only two had come from companies in other industries, and only seven (including the two from other industries) out of the 32 officers had been with more than one company. These results support Roberts' comments regarding the limited degree of mobility of executives, the great majority reaching their positions from within, after long periods of service. To the extent that this is so, the pay of a new top executive could be expected to reflect the wage and salary structure of the company, and thus internal factors, such as the number of layers of organization.

But there is another kind of evidence, also bearing on the market situation for executives, that is provided in certain of the employment contracts that are agreed to between top executives and the largest corporations. One can cite the contract made in 1936 by American Smelting and Refining with one of its vice presidents.[5] This contract assured to the executive, in addition to a $75,000 salary, the right to participate in any mining venture undertaken by the company. Similar to this are the deferred cash payments under contract which we discussed in Chapter III. For example, Chrysler made a contract with an executive which assured him of $300,000 a year as chairman of the board, and $75,000 a year for the rest of his life after retirement. In return, the executive agreed to render certain advisory and consulting services, and not to take other employment or render services to others than Chrysler without the company's consent.[6]

The significance of these contracts is that they are custom tailored to the needs of the individual executive. They are unrelated to the operation of internal company factors, such as the number of layers in an organization, cited by Roberts. They suggest, on the contrary, what Sanders describes as the "competition among corporations for the limited supply of executive ability."[7] It is a case of supply and demand in a rather elite

5. See Chapter V, p. 101.
6. Form 8-K, March 1951, Exhibit "A."
7. Sanders, *loc. cit.*

seller's market, and it can be assumed that the seller is well aware of what rival firms are offering (the absolute dollar levels cited by Roberts) for his services.

Thus there emerges from the present study a picture of a market for the top executive's services that reflects elements of truth in both the Roberts and Sanders views.

As to the effect of the small mobile group on the market for executive ability, two additional points can be made. One is that even the threat of outside competition has in fact induced some companies to make changes in their compensation arrangements for top officers. Mere dissatisfaction within the ranks of the upper echelon can bring this to pass without any actual overt move, such as the departure of a key man. However, an opposite point can be raised. Special arrangements for a new top man coming into a firm can be and often are tailored to the individual in such a way that when he departs his particular pay arrangement leaves with him, permitting the rest of the firm's internal executive pay structure to remain largely unaffected. Evidence that this may happen is adduced from the wide disparity in top executive pay for different companies.

The type of disparity that has puzzled many observers is the kind not explainable by size. Livingston raised this point in looking at corporations in many different lines of activity.[8] In relation to the 25 largest manufacturing companies, the point can be restated in this form: why should Bethlehem Steel with assets of $2,195 million give its top three men in 1958 a total pay package with a value before taxes of $1,556,000, while U.S. Steel with assets of $4,436 million (or twice as much) provided its top three with a package valued at only $1,232,000?

Since both companies are in the same industry, differences such as the foregoing would not necessarily show up in a comparison between industries. Thus the Roberts' findings that differences in executive compensation between manufacturing industries are

8. J. A. Livingston, *The American Stockholder* (Philadelphia and New York: J. B. Lippincott, 1958), pp. 222–223.

not statistically significant[9] can still be valid, even though important intercompany differences do in fact exist. These differences, however, do not break cleanly along industry division lines, and, over the long run, size of the package alone does not appear to be the controlling feature. The nature of the pay package was found in our study to be at least as important. These two matters are not unrelated.

The year-by-year historical review in Chapter VI of changes in the types of top executive compensation paid by different companies revealed the way in which a few companies exhibited highly individualistic pay patterns, which tended not only to persist but to attract "satellites" in the sense of having other companies adopt the same plan. The study of five selected companies having "satellite"-attracting plans revealed a certain historical permanence to their plans. It seems likely that the persistence of these plans explains many of the intercompany discrepancies as to the amount of the total pay package, even though the order of size of pay packages among companies varies from year to year. This is particularly true when the package includes option gains.

Differences in the make-up of the top executive pay packages for individual companies were shown to be important in the short run because they affected the size of the after-tax package. In this way intercompany differences in ranking before, contrasted with after taxes, were explained.

Discussion of long-run trends in executive pay has been characterized by three areas of agreement. The first relates to the downward trend in executive pay after allowing for taxes and the cost of living. The second has to do with the limited or short-run effects of this trend on executive performance. And the third concerns the much greater seriousness with which possible longer-run effects are viewed.

Sanders has summarized the nature of the downward trend as follows:

9. Roberts, *op. cit.*, p. 42.

The influence of high tax levels upon executive compensation is inseparable from the influence of the rise in price levels, with which it has largely been concomitant. The broad effect of the two combined has been to set up a general and sustained but largely unsuccessful, effort to offset their inroads upon the executive's standard of living by various forms of increase in his compensation.[10]

Lasser and Rothschild, writing a few years later, stated that it was impossible to provide an executive with the amount of salary increase necessary to give him a level of disposable income after taxes even as large as 50 per cent of what he was paid in 1939 or 1940.[11]

As to the second point, about the short-term effect of the supposed trend, Sanders, writing in 1951, indicated that any reduction in executives' work or effort was much exaggerated[12] and that in fact executives were working as hard as ever and were likely to continue doing so.[13] He attributed this to the way in which the disciplines of a company organization tend to keep the executive concentrated upon those opportunities which lie within his firm, and that this prevented any serious diversion of work or energies.[14]

With regard to the third point about the longer-run effects of the apparent trend, Sanders, although aiming his remarks specifically at the effects of taxation reported on

the wide prevalence of the belief that the levels and trends of taxes are likely to do serious damage in the long run to the economic structure in general and to executive performance in particular, a belief which was generally expressed by the executives interviewed. This larger question is by no means answered in a finding that executives are currently working as hard as ever.[15]

Sanders visualized the longer-run "damage" to executive performance as coming about in two different ways. First, he felt

10. Sanders, *op. cit.,* p. 85.
11. Lasser and Rothschild, *op. cit.,* p. 94.
12. Sanders, *op. cit.,* p. 12.
13. *Ibid.,* p. 76.
14. *Ibid.,* p. 19.
15. *Ibid.,* p. 17.

that the general enlargement of government in business tended to divert a substantial part of the executive's energies into economically unproductive channels (for example, the extra time devoted to tax matters).[16] Second, a reduction of executive compensation in business would gradually reduce the amount of executive ability going into business. However, he found no clear evidence that this had already occurred to a significant extent.[17]

The findings of our study are important in regard to all three of these points. Insofar as the 25 largest companies are concerned, the findings would appear to be in agreement as to much of what has happened in the past, but they raise doubts concerning the shape of the future trend.

In Chapter VI, the average pay package (including major fringes) of the three highest paid executives for all 25 companies in the sample was plotted for the 1929–1958 period. As noted there, the over-all movement was a rise of more than 60 per cent before taxes, barely any increase at all afterwards, and a decrease of more than 40 per cent if both taxes and the cost of living are taken into account. It was found in Chapter VI that, while subject to qualifications cited earlier, the before-tax pay of professional groups has probably advanced more rapidly than that for top executives.

On the basis of past performance, one guess as to the future would be that the average pay of the top executive will continue to show vigorous advance before taxes, little advance after taxes, and a decrease when both taxes and the cost of living are considered. This trend picture is a distinct possibility. Yet doubts arise. It was shown in Diagram 15 that the after-tax average was falling from 1929 until 1942. But the movement since 1942 has been upward, even after allowing for the cost of living increase. Moreover, the movement in 1955–1956 suggested a capability of reaching much higher levels. These higher levels might be achieved through executives' exercising of

16. *Ibid.*, p. 76.
17. *Ibid.*, p. 79.

options. It is also well to bear in mind that some of the earlier, more pessimistic comments about the outlook for executive pay, such as those of Sanders, were made before the impact of stock options had been fully effective. It was pointed out in Chapter VI that the average pay figure for 1958 may have been exceptionally low due to the recession, and it appears that future exercise of options already granted could boost pay trends in the future and even reverse the probable lag in the rate of advance of top executive pay compared to that for professional occupations.[18] Which of the two possible trends will prevail could be determined by legislation with respect to taxes.

Findings of the present study with regard to the second major point about the short-run effects of the trend of executive pay are partly of a negative character. There has been no evidence that would cast doubt upon the validity of the Sanders comment about executives working as hard as ever.

Adverse trends in top executive pay over the shorter run need not, of course, necessarily result in a lessening of executive effort. We might expect executive behavior to be affected in other ways such as in a tendency toward earlier retirement or increased mobility between companies. Yet, as was seen in Chapter III, there has been no significant movement toward earlier retirement among executives in the 25 largest manufacturing corporations.

With regard to the question of mobility, it was noted earlier in discussion of the market for executives that mobility of top officers in the sample has been limited. Not yet considered, however, is what has happened to mobility over a longer period of time. Has it increased, possibly reflecting executives' dissatisfaction with pay? Or has it actually decreased? The results of

18. Aside from options, as pointed out in Chapter V, top executives receive substantial income benefits through executive expense accounts. However, this was shown to be at least in part a function of the corporate income tax level. With these levels below both World War II and Korean War levels, it is doubtful if it can be argued that the trend of executive expense accounts has been upward since about 1951. In any case, the point is not readily ascertainable because of the lack of quantitative information.

the present study, although indirect in that mobility itself is not measured, are nonetheless revealing. The facts for the 176 executives in the present study for whom definite information on the length of service was available are indicated in Table 9.

Table 9—Length of Service, 176 Top Executives

Years of Service	SERVICE ENDED 1929–1943	1944–1958	Total
Less than 5	1	—	1
5 to 9	2	—	2
10 to 14	5	2	7
15 to 19	5	9	14
20 to 24	5	6	11
25 to 29	6	12	18
30 to 34	7	23	30
35 to 39	10	15	25
40 to 44	10	21	31
45 to 49	5	18	23
50 to 54	2	5	7
55 to 59	1	4	5
60 to 64	—	2	2
All Executives	59	117	176

For purposes of analysis, the totals have been broken down between executives leaving the service of one of the 25 largest companies in the period 1929–1943 and those leaving in the years 1944–1958. Now, if over the entire period mobility of these executives has increased, we should expect to see a shortening in length of service. If, on the other hand, there has been a decrease in mobility, it will be reasonable to expect an increase in length of service. In order to test what has actually taken place, the data were combined into three groupings: executives with fewer than 30 years of service, those with 30 to 44 years, and those with 45 or more years of service. Comparing the two periods of time, there was found to be no statistically significant change in the length of service for executives in the sample.[19]

This finding suggests strongly that mobility of top executives, at least among the 25 largest manufacturing companies, has

19. Application of a chi-square test showed that the difference in length of service between the two periods could have happened by chance, assuming a 5 per cent level of significance.

187

neither increased nor decreased over the 1929 to 1958 period. Thus, if there has been dissatisfaction by top executives with their pay, it has not resulted in increased mobility.

As to the longer-range effects of the apparent trend in executive pay, Sanders raised two different points, one relating to diversion of executive effort into uneconomic activities and the other with respect to a reduction in the amount of executive ability going into business. Regarding the former, the present study reveals nothing that is new. It can be observed, however, that the very proliferation of items in the top officer's pay package compared to 1929 is evidence of growth of unproductive economic activity in the form of lawyers, accountants, and other specialists who have been hired to dream up new compensation devices in order to minimize taxes. Consultations with these specialists consume more top executive energy than in earlier times.

With regard to Sanders' other point about the longer run, it would appear that the findings with respect to retirement and mobility which have already been discussed would apply also to the longer-run outlook. It is true, of course, that the faster rate of advance of professional pay, for example, if it continued for a long period, could conceivably raise such pay to levels above that for industry top executives, thus affecting the supply of ability going into industry. But as long as the top executive cannot be paid more in any alternative occupation, as appears now to be the case, the possibility considered does not seem likely to become a reality.

After considering the significance of the over-all trends in the average pay of the top executive in industry, we now turn our attention to the findings with respect to differentials among the top three.

The findings of Chapter VIII showed that the dollar margin before taxes of the first highest paid executive over the second tended to move in the same direction as the curve for average pay. That is, the tendency was to shrink in depression and to widen in prosperity. The same was true of the dollar margin of the second highest officer over the third.

The tendency cited appears to result from both the cyclical movement of profits and stock prices and the effects of these movements on nonsalary items in the top executive pay package, such as bonuses and option gains. To the extent that bonuses and option grants are made in proportion to pay, the mechanical result is to shrink or expand the pre-tax dollar (but not necessarily percentage) differentials. This assumes no change in salary structure, but, of course, salaries may also rise. So long, however, as the rise is a percentage increase rather than an across-the-board increase, the general result is likely to be in the same direction. Evidence from personnel practices with regard to top executive salaries is that both increases and decreases typically take the form of percentage changes.

If percentage rather than dollar differentials are traced, however, movements appear to exhibit a more obvious downward trend. Looking at the situation before taxes and excluding option gains, the margin of the highest paid executive dropped from 75 per cent to 42 per cent over the 1929–1958 period. For the second man the percentage dropped from 29 per cent to 13 per cent.

With respect to option grants, it must be pointed out that, although grants are likely to be in proportion to salary, the evidence has shown that this is not necessarily true of exercise of options.

Now a significant fact noted in Chapter VIII is that option gains, when included in differentials, have tended sometimes to reinforce them and sometimes to eliminate them entirely. As in the case of the top executive's average pay, the outlook for the future has been viewed as involving two possible alternatives— narrower and narrower percentage margins, or, by contrast, a reversal in the direction of wider differentials. The latter possibility was related to grant as opposed to exercise of options. Shares granted are typically in proportion to the executive's ranking in the organization, or to his before-tax pay excluding options. Thus the grants are designed to reinforce differentials. Also, we have seen that the before-tax average for the three highest paid officers together rose more than 60 per cent over the 1929–1958 period. Excluding options, the rise was still impressive. Thus in the future, exercise of options already granted could enlarge differentials among the three top officers. But again, as was true for the average top officer's pay, the outcome appeared to depend on tax legislation.

Percentage differentials in 1958, still excluding options, but taking the data after taxes, were 29 per cent for the top officer and approximately 10 per cent for the second man. These data are interesting because the top man's margin for the 25 companies as a whole is not too much above the 25 per cent minimum cited by Greenewalt as necessary between successive layers of organization,[20] and by this standard the second man no longer had his head above water. This naturally evokes questions: If, say, 10 per cent is inadequate, does an executive put up with such a situation as being temporary? What size of percentage differential is really needed? Or indeed, would not dollar differentials of some size adequately serve the purpose and if so what size? Such questions provide a large area for future research.

Aside from absolute percentage or dollar standards, the importance of what has happened can be evaluated in relation to the effects on executive performance and on mobility. As to performance, the Sanders finding mentioned earlier that executives are still working as hard as ever and are likely to continue to do so would appear to apply again. With regard to mobility, we saw earlier that most top executives are promoted from within. As to the small amount of mobility that does exist, however, Hall reports that reduced differentials have had little effect on the power of the larger companies to attract able executives.[21]

Speaking of the contents of the executive pay package, John C. Baker, writing in 1938, had this to say about how executives in the larger industrial companies were paid: "There are basically

20. See Chapter VIII, p. 165.
21. Hall, *op. cit.*, p. 263.

190

. . . only two methods of paying executives: salary, and salary and some form of bonus, with variations."[22]

This statement would no longer be a valid summary of the methods of paying top executives, particularly in the 25 largest manufacturing companies. The changes that have taken place have been analyzed in a qualitative way by various compensation specialists.[23] What our study has done is to portray a few quantitative dimensions of the changes—in terms of rates of growth and different shares of the pay package.

For the 1929–1958 period, the most significant change has been that with respect to current versus deferred payment in all its forms. Over these years current payment grew only slightly before taxes and actually shrank after taxes. By contrast, deferred payment as a whole grew. As a share of the total pay package, while deferment before taxes had a net movement from 7 per cent to more than 35 per cent, current payment declined from 93 per cent to almost 65 per cent.

The decline in the quantitative importance of current payment has not resulted in a corresponding drop in the functional importance of salaries. This is partly true because much of the decline was occasioned by the shift in bonus payments away from current payment to deferred payment. These findings were brought out in Chapter II. There are, however, other reasons.

Salaries, as was developed in Chapter I, were in 1958 still the largest single item in the top executive pay package. They have been the most stable item, at least before taxes. Moreover, they have continued to serve as status symbols. This has been evident from the study in two ways. First, even in recent years, instances were found where the chairman of the board was given the highest salary, but did not have the highest total pay package. In such cases the chairman often did not share in a bonus or an option grant. In the second place, major fringe benefits have tended to reinforce status patterns indicated by differences in

22. Baker, *op. cit.*, p. 186.
23. For a fairly typical discussion along these lines see Lasser and Rothschild, *op. cit.*

salary. This applies to pensions, thrift plan benefits, grant (but not exercise) of options, and often even to bonuses. The continuing importance of salaries for executives has been remarked upon by Lasser and Rothschild,[24] Martucci, [25] and others.

Among our findings on bonuses are that the largest companies related bonus payments to profits by formula more than was the case in earlier years, and that the interest of the stockholder appears to be better protected by specific provisions in bonus plans. These findings point to a more rational, less arbitrary approach, to the equitable distribution of company profits than was true in 1929. Nevertheless, it was also found that for 1958 the size of bonus payments, if the Smyth standard is accepted,[26] was for some firms overgenerous when compared to salaries, while in other companies bonuses were found to be so small as to provide little incentive.

With regard to the GM plan which provides for short-term deferment, Hall states that the short period of deferment—only five years—"was adopted in part to prevent the plan from becoming a symbol of involuntary servitude."[27] This would seem to indicate that GM's management wished to avoid a perhaps more extreme holding effect on its executives, which might have resulted from longer deferment.

Kingman Brewster raises the matter of the holding effect in even stronger terms:

There can be no dispute about the tendency of many compensation and retirement schemes to hold executives . . . within the "jurisdiction" of the corporation in which they first choose to reside. Indeed that is usually their purpose. Deferred compensation and stock-warrant and retirement plans with a "you can't take it with you" feature seem to be successful in their purpose of reducing the horizontal mobility of talent.[28]

24. *Ibid.*, p. 102.
25. Nicholas L. A. Martucci, "Problems in Executive Salary Determination," *Management Record*, XVII (January 1955), pp. 9–11.
26. See Chapter II, p. 43.
27. Hall, *op. cit.*, p. 145.
28. Kingman Brewster in *The Corporation in Modern Society*, Edward S. Mason, ed. (Cambridge: Harvard University Press, 1959), p. 78.

In sharp contrast to the above Roberts quotes one company officer as conceding

that substantial unvested rights to deferred compensation are a deterrent, other things being equal, but . . . if the new company really wants the man, it offers to make good his loss so that in practice there is little deterrent effect.[29]

Two findings in our study have a bearing in relation to the holding effect of short-term deferment. During the 1929–1958 period, the number of companies among the 25 largest having such plans increased from two[30] to about six. And yet, as pointed out earlier, there was no significant change in the length of service over this period for the top executives sampled. Any decrease in mobility would supposedly be reflected in an increased length of service.

Our findings support the generally held belief that short-term deferment offers a useful device for providing a more even distribution of income, dampening the fluctuations arising out of good and bad years in terms of profit. The findings do not, however, indicate any tax advantage for the short-term deferment scheme except under certain conditions which were explained in Chapter VII. It was also pointed out that for the 25-company sample this method of payment actually resulted in a higher per cent of tax than was true for current payment.

Another interesting conclusion, developed in Chapter VI, is that over the 1929–1958 period there was a close race between short-term and postretirement deferment, with the former falling behind slightly on an after-tax basis in recent years.

The tax advantage of postretirement deferment to the executive has been couched in these terms by Livingston: "By deferring his compensation—by charging his services to latter-day stockholders and consumers—he gets pay for past services when his income tax bracket drops."[31] Our findings are that the reference

29. Roberts, *op. cit.,* p. 131.

30. Although two companies had such plans in 1929, only one company shows up in the present study, because GM did not report its 1929 compensation data to the FTC.

31. Livingston, *op. cit.,* p. 230.

to a drop in income tax bracket does not hold as true as is commonly thought. There is, as was shown in Chapter VII, a demonstrable advantage where the total income stream is substantially reduced, as is typically the case for pensions and deferred cash payments under contract. But for postretirement stock bonus plans, such as that of GE, actual calculations indicate that the tax advantage is substantially offset by accumulations of stock and dividends, which add to postretirement income.

Capital gains tax treatment of rapidly growing thrift plan benefits, combined with the postretirement deferment advantages of pensions and deferred cash payments under contract, would appear to be enough, regardless of the lesser tax advantage of the GE type of stock bonus, to account for the recent after-tax pulling ahead of postretirement deferment in contrast to short-term deferment.

As contrasted, however, with current payment, postretirement deferment has grown far more rapidly over the 1929–1958 period, and the largest item in postretirement deferment has been the income value of pensions. This raises a question as to whether the trend to postretirement deferment, and especially pensions, has had the effect of causing executives to retire earlier. One of the findings of the present study, described in Chapter III, is that, for the executives in the 25-company sample, there was no significant difference in retirement age for executives retiring in 1929–1943 in contrast to 1944–1958. (For the entire period the typical retirement age was sixty-five.) This finding, for executives in the 25 largest companies, gives concrete factual support to the general opinion reported by Roberts. Hall, though apparently detecting some evidence of earlier retirement "in one or two cases reviewed," has offered reasons why this result was not likely to be widespread:

1. Non-financial incentives are important to most executives, particularly those in top positions and retirement means the loss of power,[32] prestige, and a sense of achievement.

---

32. For a discussion of the power of management, see Mason, ed., *op. cit.*, especially the article by Carl Kaysen.

2. Retirement usually occasions a sharp drop in income which many executives attempt to postpone by prolonging employment.

3. The terms of most deferred compensation plans do not encourage early retirement.[33]

The present study is not at variance with the above, except in one instance. With regard to the second point, there is a corollary to the earlier proposition about the lesser tax-minimizing effect of postretirement deferred stock bonuses. The corollary is that the postretirement drop in income is, at least for firms numbered among the 25 largest, typically well cushioned. As for the holding effect of postretirement deferment, it may be somewhat greater than for short-term deferment, but in general the points already made in connection with short-term deferment would seem to apply here.

The chief other type of deferment, flexible deferment, as used in the present study has been confined to stock option and purchase gains. In a broader sense, this is only one kind of flexible deferment. Differences in personal and family needs could indicate another kind of flexibility. Arthur F. Burns has found that young married couples are the only age group in the population which is a net debtor group.[34] Even though relating to a group younger than the executives included here, this finding points up the way in which the economic needs of younger men differ from those of older men. The latter, who have become more successful, may need less money currently and prefer to take it after retirement. This would argue for greater flexibility in payment, allowing the executive to take his pay as he wishes. Lasser and Rothschild have suggested the desirability of a plan allowing an executive to take compensation either currently or in deferred payment.[35] Some instances of this approach have been found in our study. Individual arrangements under employment contracts often reflect this type of thinking. In IBM, for in-

33. Hall, as quoted in Roberts, *op. cit.*, p. 188n.
34. Arthur F. Burns, *Prosperity Without Inflation* (New York: Fordham University Press, 1957), p. 21.
35. Lasser and Rothschild, *op. cit.*, p. 102.

stance, two out of the top three executives in recent years have received salaries and a currently paid bonus. The third executive gets a bonus equal in amount to that of one of the other two officers, but payable on a short-term deferment basis. He is scheduled to receive each such bonus over a ten-year period following the year of award.

Flexible deferment in the narrower sense, including stock option and purchase gains, has been analyzed in detail in Chapter IV. It was seen that for the 25 largest companies, most of the unrealized capital gains resulting from the exercise of options took place in the years 1952–1958, and that the amounts showed marked instability ranging from extreme high to extreme low levels. A question which may be raised is whether such movements have a significance in connection with the business cycle. Do such extreme variations in purchases of stock under option tend to have undersirable effects on stock prices, which may in turn have further repercussions?

The recent unfavorable findings of the Division of Corporate Regulation of the SEC, with respect to the impact of options on the market price of stock for electric utilities, are borne out only in part by our study, at least insofar as the Division's findings would apply to any of the 25 largest manufacturing companies having options. The conclusion of the present study was that the market price is affected greatly by external factors (as the Division maintained), but also in some degree by internal manipulation (a matter on which confidential interview material was utilized), and to a lesser extent by the executive's performance. The Division also found an unfavorable effect on company earnings. It would be worth further investigation to find out whether the same would be true of manufacturing companies.

Aside from the speculative aspects of option gains, it was shown in Chapter IV how such devices as "puts,"[36] contingent credits, and dividend units could be used to protect option-holding executives from loss in case of a market decline. Still

36. See Chapter IV, p. 76.

other aspects of option gains have been brought out in various chapters. In Chapter VIII it was seen that option gains sometimes reinforce but at other times completely wipe out differentials among the three highest paid executives. This raises a question of policy: is it desirable that a form of compensation have the effect of sometimes eliminating differentials in a sporadic and rather unpredictable manner? Is this a move in the direction of a more rational pay structure, or is it really irrational? On the other hand, in Chapter VI it was shown that the average pay package of the top executive has increased in recent years much more than it would have in the absence of option gains, even assuming the substantial year-to-year changes in the amounts of the gains. Finally, Chapter VII, and especially the discussion of Diagram 28, showed that the tax treatment of stock option gains is extremely favorable to the top executive. As put by J. Keith Butters: "The preferential treatment given to capital gains in general constitutes another way—probably the single most important way—in which the full impact of the individual income tax rates is avoided."[37]

All of the above considerations would seem to suggest a fundamental paradox whose only real solution may be legislative. Taxes aside, there seem to be a great many questionable aspects of stock options, not the least of which is that they are far from an ideal method of compensation in the sense of relating reward to effort. And yet, as the law is written, the tax advantage to the executive is extremely powerful. On this subject Norman S. Cannon has observed:

It would not be difficult to quarrel with past Congressional action in the field of executive compensation. For example, why should the restricted stock option be singled out for action instead of a sound executive type of deferred profit-sharing plan?[38]

37. J. Keith Butters, Laurence E. Thompson, and Lynn L. Bollinger, *Effects of Taxation—Investments by Individuals* (Boston: Graduate School of Business Administration, Harvard University, 1953), p. 82.
38. Norman S. Cannon, "Some Selected Problems in Accounting for Executive Compensation" (unpublished Ph.D. dissertation, Graduate School of Business, Columbia University), p. 204.

SEC Regulations and Tax Policies

In this study we have been much concerned with SEC Regulations, and with tax policies of the federal government. In the first place, the study would probably have been impossible without the detailed information concerning executive compensation, which SEC makes available. In the second, federal taxes, both on individual incomes and on capital gains, constitute one of the most important factors influencing the historical movement of the top executive's pay package. Here, we wish to comment on changes which might be desirable both in the regulations and in tax legislation as they apply to executives' pay.

Because the Annual Reports, Form 10-K, and annual proxy statements required by the Securities and Exchange Commission are the most important single source of publicly available information on the remuneration of corporate top executives, the reporting requirements laid down by this agency deserve careful scrutiny. There are at least two respects in which they need improvement. One is in the reporting of stock option benefits; the other concerns pensions.

The reporting to SEC by corporations with respect to stock options has been criticized by Griswold in the following terms:

The notice and information now available to shareholders, particularly with respect to the exercise of options and the extent of the benefits obtained, does not now seem to be adequate.[39]

In the discussion in Chapter IV, it was brought out that the information on options as reported in proxy statements consisted mostly of details, from which it was necessary for the reader to go through a computation process in order to find out what the unrealized capital gains were at the time of exercise of the options. And there was no information at all as to realized gains. In other words, it was left to the compensation specialist to put the pieces together, if he could. In order to make avail-

39. U.S. SEC, Division of Corporate Regulation, *op. cit.,* Appendix F.

able a public record that reveals more adequately the facts on stock option benefits, we would recommend that for all employees whose compensation is reported by name to the SEC, the following should be made available in annual proxy statements:

1. The actual dollar amounts of unrealized capital gains at the time of exercise. This should include gains for both present and retired employees on any options granted during the preceding ten years.

2. At the time of sale of stock purchased under option, the dollar amounts of the realized capital gains. Again, this should include not only present but also retired employees who were granted options at any time during the past ten years.

3. As to current information, the reporting period on stock options should be identical with that used for other types of remuneration—the company's fiscal year.

4. Details of the prices of options and market prices at time of purchase or sale, and number of shares, etc., should be omitted from proxy statements, because they are unnecessary. However, these details should be maintained by reporting firms and reported on Form 4's to the SEC.

On the third point, present SEC Regulations require the reporting of the exercise of options for a period which does not coincide with that for other types of remuneration. The pertinent regulation is:

Furnish the following information as to all options to purchase securities, from the issuer or any of its subsidiaries, which were granted to or exercised by the following persons *since the beginning of the issuer's last fiscal year....*[40]

This provision results in reporting of shares, for example, for the period January 1, 1956, through March 15, 1957. Not only does this disagree with the period for which salary and other pay elements are reported, but it creates an overlap period between

40. U.S. SEC, *General Rules and Regulations under the Securities Exchange Act of 1934,* as in effect January 10, 1958, Schedule 14A, Item 7(d). Italics added.

years, which is misleading and confusing to the general public.

SEC Regulations in effect during 1958 concerning the reporting of pensions called for the estimated annual benefits upon retirement for each of the three highest paid officers, but added: "The information called for . . . may be given in a table showing the annual benefits payable upon retirement to persons in specified salary classifications."[41] In other words, if the pension figures were going to look pretty high, the company would not be obliged to show them for the top three men. It could conceal such payments by using the table instead.

In 1958, 15 out of 25 reporting companies showed estimated pension benefits for each of the three highest paid officers, while nine firms showed no such figures, and one concern indicated only the amount of the pension paid for by the company. The nine firms that furnished no information for the top three men showed instead a schedule of pensions assuming different salary levels and years of service. The nine companies employing this device (which under the present regulations they have every legal right to do), included: Bethlehem Steel, Du Pont, GM, Socony, Standard Oil of Indiana, Standard Oil of California, Standard Oil of New Jersey, Union Carbide, and U.S. Steel.

In the light of the many inadequacies of present pension reporting in indicating the extent of retirement benefits actually received, or expected to be received in the future, by the highest paid corporate executives, it is recommended that the permissive feature of showing a schedule of salaries and pensions for given periods of service be abolished. Companies would thus again be required to show for at least each of the three highest paid officers the amounts of estimated pension benefits to be paid at retirement. Such estimates, although based on somewhat unrealistic assumptions as pointed out earlier, at least provide a minimum of usable information with regard to top executive pension benefits.

In the matter of federal tax policies, we may recall how various devices have been used for minimizing taxes on top executive compensation. This was explored in Chapter VII,

41. *Ibid.*, Item 7(b), par. 3 of instructions.

and to a lesser degree in Chapter V. Among the devices were deductions analyzed in Chapter V that were taken before determination of adjusted gross income and fell into the category of executive expense accounts or business deductions. In Chapter VII we examined deductions from adjusted gross income, or personal deductions. Our study offers no evidence that either type of deduction has had any effect on the make-up of the executive pay package, but both types affect the executive's performance.

Business deductions in the form of tax-free executive expense accounts were seen in Chapter V to have been fostered by the idea of "cheap dollars" arising out of a high level of corporate income tax. To the extent that such expenses do not serve a true business purpose, they may involve either a weakening in the quality of the executive's performance or a diversion of his energies. Two remedies would be a tightening up on expense account abuses, and a drastic lowering of the corporate income tax rate.[42] A question worth further investigation is whether reporting of expense account data for top officers to the SEC might also serve to restrain abuses.

In Chapter VII, we saw that personal deductions as a per cent of income tended to rise as adjusted gross income rose. They have had a dampening effect on the tax rate curve, because lower rates applied than otherwise would be the case. To the extent that the tax rates have an unfavorable effect, personal deductions, since they partly offset this, probably have a favorable influence on executive performance. It follows that changes in the law, which would further limit the itemizing of personal deductions, would (at least on the grounds of the result for executive performance) be undesirable.[43]

Another of the devices has been the effective tax rate curve. Differences both over time and between income levels as reflected in the tax rate curve have been utilized to minimize taxes.

42. A congressman's view on this latter point was cited before. See Chapter V, p. 105.
43. In any case it is clear that an attempt to place tighter over-all restraints on them could produce unwanted side effects, such, for example, as reducing the flow of private contributions into educational institutions.

In Chapter VII we saw that over the 1929–1958 period the impact of taxes on major elements of the top executive pay package varied. Least impact was obtained through flexible deferment, which avoided the high progressive rates altogether. But even among elements subject to the full rates (or mostly so), marked differences were apparent. The effective rate curve, at least with its present high rates, favors postretirement pensions and to a lesser extent postretirement bonuses, and penalizes not only currently paid but also short-term deferred bonuses.

The results of federal tax policy in this regard are longer-run than may be thought at first glance. Currently paid bonuses have, as shown in Chapter II, suffered a long-run decline in relative importance since 1929. Although short-term deferment has risen, as indicated in Chapter VI, the total for all forms of postretirement deferment has already pulled ahead of short-term deferment after taxes. Thus the portent of the future is an even greater tendency toward postretirement deferment. This trend too, however, has not had a net result of inducing top executives in the largest companies to retire earlier to make more room at the top for younger executives.

As to the two tax-penalized forms of compensation—current payment and short-term deferment—it can be said that both have an advantage not possessed, for example, by a postretirement bonus plan such as that of GE. This advantage is that they relate reward to effort more closely in time. These and other nontax considerations could be given more weight in setting of company policies, if it were not for the present high tax rates on upper income brackets.

Not only does the rate curve affect the way in which an executive is paid, it also has considerable bearing on his performance. As to what has been happening, a former Treasury official, Dan T. Smith, put it this way:

With high taxes, it becomes much more important to save a dollar of taxes than to earn another dollar of income. At a 90% tax rate, it is 10 times as important to save a dollar of taxes as to earn a dollar of income. This fact cannot do other than divert attention from production to tax minimization

—an activity which involves perhaps the most flagrant sort of conflict between private and social net products.[44]

That this shift of emphasis from production to tax minimization may not be minor in its effect on the quality of top executive performance can be seen from the remarks of the president of a large industrial company, cited by Butters:

> I sometimes wonder whether one of the most serious effects of taxation . . . may not be the amount of time and energy consumed in the weighing of these effects by a great multitude of individuals. The energy spent in the efforts to adapt, accommodate, avoid, or even evade, must be great. If these same energies would be directed into more productive channels, they would add up to something like the power of an atomic explosion. I sometimes think that the simplification of the tax structure, combined with the reduction of the tax burden, would release enough energy to provide more than enough offsetting income.[45]

To remedy the undesirable effects produced by the tax rate structure, a drastic reduction in upper income tax rates is proposed. The small revenue effects of large reductions in the upper brackets, in contrast to the larger effects of small reductions in lower brackets, have already been pointed out. Specifically, we saw in Chapter VII that abolition of all progression in rates above 50 per cent would only cost around $800 million, or less than 2 per cent of $40 billion of revenue collected.[46] In order to encourage more flexibility in choice of executive pay plans, and also to improve the quality of executive performance, a drastic reduction in upper income tax rates should be accompanied by removal of special tax treatment of other forms of income, such as certain types of capital gains.

Butters was quoted earlier as saying that capital gains treatment of income was the major way in which the full impact of individual income tax rates was avoided.[47] This has been amply supported by the findings in Chapter VII with regard to stock

44. Smith, *op. cit.*, p. 66.
45. Butters, *op. cit.*, p. 49.
46. See Chapter VII, p. 149.
47. See this chapter, p. 197.

option gains. We have seen that if all the tax-minimizing devices are grouped together, management's success in blunting the effects of fully progressive rates increased markedly from 1952 on,[48] precisely the period when stock options became an important share of the top officer's pay package. When the tax effect on different elements of the pay package was traced over the 1929–1958 period, flexible deferment showed the lowest tax rate.

We have already reviewed (Chapter VII) charges by Griswold and others that stock options are discriminatory.[49] There, two points were made: First, it was indicated that other plans, such as those of GM and GE, are likewise discriminatory in the sense of not being qualified under treasury regulations. Second, it was indicated that stock option plans are really adopted, at least in part, to offset what many top executives feel is discrimination against them in the form of excessively high individual income tax rates.

As we know, still other aspects of stock options leave room for serious doubt about the desirability of options as a compensation device.

Weighing tax against nontax factors, the following is recommended: do away with special capital gains treatment of stock option benefits, leaving all such income fully taxable to the extent of the excess of the market value over the option value, at the time the option is exercised. Assuming that rates on upper income brackets are reduced at the same time, an advantage of the change in law on options would be to encourage companies again to rely more on profit-sharing and bonus plans, which relate reward more closely to effort.[50]

A way other than stock option benefits in which capital gains rates serve to hold taxes to a minimum, is by means of thrift

48. See Chapter VII, Diagram 26.
49. See Chapter VII, p. 161.
50. For an example of critical discussion of stock options, see Erwin N. Griswold, "Are Stock Options Getting Out of Hand?" *Harvard Business Review*, XXXVIII, No. 6 (1960), pp. 49–55.

plans. The rapid growth of such plans, mentioned in Chapter III, is witness to the manner in which the tax provision has acted. Such plans, as well as lump sum distributions under pension plans, seem likely to continue to grow rapidly in the future. These methods of compensation, in contrast to stock option plans, are not discriminatory in the sense of favoring top executives. They make it possible for not only the top officer but also the average worker to incur a large capital expense at retirement—such as the purchase of a home—without the lump sum payment being heavily depleted. This depletion would of course affect even the average employee, if the lump sum payment were fully taxable in the year received. Thrift plans also encourage savings, which helps to stimulate economic growth.

It has been demonstrated in Chapter III that thrift plans still represent only a small share of the top executive pay package. There is no evidence in the present study that they have had an undesirable effect on how executives are paid or on executive performance. Thus there appears no compelling reason to change the present capital gains treatment of thrift plan benefits. In fact, arguments in their favor point the other way.

The other tax-minimizing device utilized by management is the dividend credit. In connection with top executive pay, we have seen in Chapter VII that this device is at present of relatively minor importance. For the future, however, it appears that the Du Pont scheme of dividend units has set a pattern likely to be adopted by others among the largest companies, as long as the credit remains in the law. From a company policy viewpoint, (aside from tax minimization) there seems to be little justification for favoring dividends over other forms of executive compensation. Consistent with our recommendations on stock option gains, removal of the credit would place all forms of executive compensation on a more equal footing.[51]

51. No attempt is made here to evaluate the dividend credit on grounds other than those specifically relating to executive compensation. For an analysis of the double taxation of dividends and other aspects of the 1954 legislation, see Carl S. Shoup, "The Dividend Exclusion and Credit in the Revenue Code of 1954," *National Tax Journal*, VIII, No. 1 (March, 1955), pp. 136–137.

The Distribution of Income by Occupation

Finally, there remains to be answered one other question of importance: is it possible that the income going to top executives in manufacturing industry is excessive, despite the inroads of taxes, the rising cost of living, and so on? Are pay rates for top executives such that they attract the ablest men out of other essential occupations to the detriment of society?

A few of the facts can be gleaned by looking at how the pay of executives in manufacturing compares with that for leaders in other occupations. In 1958, the median salary of the third highest paid executive for the 25 largest manufacturing companies was $113,000. The median salary for the president of a private university was $25,000, and that for a full professor was $9,000.[52] The salary of the Secretary of Defense is fixed by law at $25,000.[53]

In addition to these facts about salaries, it is interesting to look at one of the more important fringes. Again taking the third highest paid executive in our study, the median pension, taken from estimates reported in proxy statements,[54] was $44,000.

Despite the before-tax basis of comparison used here and questions which can be raised about differences in job content, certain conclusions can be drawn from the numerical evidence. We can see that pay levels of industrial top executives are not merely higher than those for leaders in education or in government. They are multiples of the latter, and even pensions are estimated in many cases as being higher in industry than what leaders in education and government are paid for working. These comparisons yield preliminary evidence of a greater need for

52. 11–12 Month Salaries, from W. Robert Bokelman, *Higher Education Planning and Management Data,* U.S. Department of Health, Education, and Welfare Circular No. 549 (Washington: U.S. Government Printing Office, 1959), pp. 11, 36.

53. Livingston, *op. cit.,* pp. 234–235.

54. These are based on somewhat unrealistic assumptions, as pointed out in Chapter I, and are if anything understated.

206

further research into occupational pay differences. This is particularly true where, as in government and education, these differences may be reflected in one-way mobility out of such underpaid occupations and into higher-paying industry. Of course, future investigations of interoccupational pay differences will prove more realistic and of greater value if heavier emphasis is placed on total pay packages, including major fringe benefits, as has been attempted for top executives in this study.

APPENDIX I

Details About
Selection of Sample

For the years 1929, 1937, 1942, and 1948, A. D. H. Kaplan's lists of the 100 largest industrials were used.[1] Canadian companies and firms like Montgomery Ward and Sears Roebuck & Company, which were not primarily engaged in manufacturing, were eliminated. Then the Kaplan lists were employed in two different ways.

First, the lists for 1929 and 1948 were used to determine, in order of size according to total assets, the 25 largest manufacturing companies. The next eight largest companies were also included so as to provide substitutions if that should later prove necessary. That meant a total for each of the two years of 33 companies.

Second, lists for 1935 and 1948 were employed to obtain new lists for 1937 and 1942. A worksheet was set up for the 50 largest companies in each of the two years 1935 and 1948.

1. Kaplan, *op. cit.,* pp. 149–154.

Then new columns were set up, using *Moody's Industrial Manual*,[2] to obtain the total assets in 1937 and 1942 for every company on each of the two neighboring lists. After that, the 1937 and 1942 data were ordered by asset size, the 25 largest being selected for each year, once more with a reserve of eight companies, again making a total for each year of 33 firms. In addition to the firms in the Kaplan listings, one other company, Cities Service, which in 1929 was essentially a public utility, having less than half its gross earnings represented by oil, has been included in the list of manufacturers for 1937 and later years, reflecting the substantial change in the nature of this company's business.[3]

For 1952 and the years from 1955 to 1958, similar lists of the 25 largest (plus eight extras in reserve to total 33) were worked out using compilations of the First National City Bank or the National Industrial Conference Board.

Western Electric, since it is a subsidiary of American Telephone and Telegraph Company, and therefore does not report separately to the Securities and Exchange Commission on the pay of its top officers, was removed from the sample in all years.

Finally, all companies in each of the eight years sampled in the 1937–1958 period were checked to see if they were listed on an organized stock exchange; and nonlisted companies, which are not required to report pay information to the SEC, were taken from the list. For 1929 the firms in the tentative sample were checked directly against Federal Trade Commission records, to determine the availability of information on top executive pay.

As a result of the final check it was found that for the year 1929 only, the 33 concerns on the original list were not enough, so 3 other firms, somewhat further down on the 1929 Kaplan listing, were added.

2. *Moody's Industrial Manual,* 1937 and 1942.

3. Company records show that, although in 1929 roughly half the firm's gross earnings were from oil operations, by 1937 more than three-quarters of its total revenues came from oil.

APPENDIX II

The 25-Company Sample

The 25-Company Sample[a]

Company	'29	'37	'42	'48	'52	'55	'56	'57	'58
				YEARS INCLUDED IN STUDY					
Allied Chemical		X							
Aluminum Co. of America					X	X	X	X	X
American Smelting & Refining	X								
American Tobacco	X	X	X	X	X	X			
The Anaconda Co.	X	X	X	X	X	X	X	X	X
Armour & Co.		X	X						
Bethlehem Steel	X	X	X	X	X	X	X	X	X
Chrysler			X	X	X	X	X	X	X
Cities Service		X	X	X	X	X	X	X	X
Dow Chemical					X				
Du Pont	X	X	X	X	X	X	X	X	X
Ford						X	X	X	X
General Electric		X	X	X	X	X	X	X	X
General Motors		X	X	X	X	X	X	X	X
Goodyear Tire & Rubber	X		X		X	X	X	X	X
Gulf Oil				X	X	X	X	X	X
International Business Machines								X	X
International Harvester	X	X	X	X	X	X	X	X	X
International Paper	X	X							
Jones & Laughlin Steel	X		X						
Kennecott Copper	X	X	X	X			X		

211

Company									
Phillips Petroleum				X	X	X	X	X	X
The Pullman Co.	X	X							
Republic Steel	X	X	X	X	X	X	X	X	X
R. J. Reynolds Tobacco	X			X					
Shell Oil	X	X	X	X	X	X	X	X	X
Sinclair Oil	X	X	X	X	X	X	X	X	X
Socony Mobil Oil	X	X	X	X	X	X	X	X	X
Standard Oil (Ind.)		X	X	X	X	X	X	X	X
Standard Oil of Cal.	X	X	X	X	X	X	X	X	X
Standard Oil of N.J.	X	X	X	X	X	X	X	X	X
Swift & Co.		X	X	X					
The Texas Co.	X	X	X	X	X	X	X	X	X
Tidewater Oil	X								
Union Carbide	X	X	X	X	X	X	X	X	X
U.S. Rubber	X								
U.S. Steel	X	X	X	X	X	X	X	X	X
Westinghouse Electric	X		X	X	X	X	X	X	X
Youngstown Sheet & Tube	X	X							

* Predecessor companies represented where appropriate. See Appendix I for details about selection of sample.

APPENDIX III

The Tax Calculations

This appendix, including the examples, illustrates the nature of the calculations used in deriving the individual income tax rate curves, such as those shown in Diagram 25 and used throughout the study in arriving at rates used against taxable income before exemptions.

Significant changes can be brought about in the effective rates through changes in exemptions, income credits, tax credits, maximum rate limitations, as well as temporary extra taxes imposed in wartime, and, after the war, the income-splitting provision on joint returns. How these factors affected the final rates will be evident from examples.

For illustrative purposes only, discussion will be in terms of a $600,000 income, after deductions but before exemptions. To avoid repetition the procedure will be to describe in detail the 1929 calculations and then to detail thereafter only the changes as they affected the calculation of the tax curves.

In 1929 the net income for surtax was fully taxable, there being no surtax exemption. The bracket applicable to the $600,000 income was from $500,000 to $750,000. The tax up to the lower limit of the bracket was $91,660. The amount within the bracket was $100,000, which taxed at 20 per cent amounted to $20,000. The $91,660 plus the $20,000 gave a total surtax of $111,660.

Net income for normal tax was $600,000, against which a married couple with two dependents was allowed exemptions of $4,300, leaving a taxable income for normal tax of $595,700. The normal tax was ½ per cent of the first $4,000, 2 per cent of the next $4,000, and 4 per cent of the balance over $8,000. On this basis the normal tax worked out to $23,608.

The surtax of $111,660 plus normal tax of $23,608 totaled $135,268. From this was subtracted a tax credit amounting to 25 per cent of the surtax plus the normal tax on earned income up to $30,000. The credit in this case worked out to $422, leaving a final tax of $134,846.

The tax, divided by the net income, yielded an effective tax rate of 22.5 per cent. In Diagram 25 the appropriate point on the 1929 curve can be located, at the $600,000 taxable income level.

The situation as it existed in the 1936–1939 period reflected several changes in addition to the big advances in rates. Exemptions were smaller. But they could be subtracted not only from normal tax income but also from surtax net income. In a second change, the tax credit disappeared. In its place was a credit of 10 per cent of earned income up to $14,000, which was subtracted from net income to determine income subject to the normal tax. At the same time, the step-type normal tax was replaced by a flat 4 per cent.

In 1936 the normal tax net income of $600,000 was reduced by an earned income credit of 10 per cent of $14,000, or $1,400, and by exemptions of $3,300, to leave taxable income of $595,300. This was subject to a normal tax rate of 4 per cent, yielding a normal tax of $23,812. The surtax was arrived at by the usual method, except that the $3,300 of exemptions was subtracted before applying the surtax.

During the defense and wartime years new and temporary taxes were imposed, in addition to increasing the regular rates. These new taxes comprised the defense tax in 1940 and the victory tax in 1943.

The defense tax was 10 per cent superimposed on the total tax, but was not to be more than 10 per cent of net income less the total tax.

For the $600,000 executive the total tax in 1940 (including surtax and normal tax) was $384,652. The tentative defense tax was 10 per cent of this or $38,465. Net income less total tax was $215,348, and 10 per cent of that was $21,535, the maximum defense tax allowed. The total including the defense tax was $406,187.

The victory tax was imposed on a larger net income than the normal and surtax. After exemptions the tax was 5 per cent of victory tax net income less a special credit. Also, the tax was limited by a 90 per cent of net income roof established for the total tax including the victory tax. This limitation has continued in effect, although the level has varied somewhat.

For the $600,000 executive in 1943 victory tax net income was assumed to be ten-ninths of ordinary net income or $666,667.[1] From this was subtracted an exemption of $624 to get taxable income of $666,043. The 5 per cent tax amounted to $33,302 before credits. Assuming a married couple with two dependents, the credit was 40 per cent, plus 2 per cent for each dependent, or 44 per cent, but this was limited to a maximum of $1,200. The gross tax of $33,302 less the $1,200 credit yielded a victory tax of $32,102. This still left the executive with total taxes of less than 90 per cent of ordinary net income, so the limit did not enter the picture.

In 1944–1945 the earned income credit in effect since 1934 was eliminated. In 1946–1947 the exemptions allowable against normal tax were increased and a tax credit of 5 per cent allowed on the total of normal and surtax.

In 1948–1949 the split income provisions on joint returns came into effect. Applied tax credits of the step type were also introduced.

For the $600,000 officer in 1948 net income after a $2,400 exemption was $597,600. Following the split-income rule, this was divided by two to get $298,800. The combined normal and surtax on this amount was $246,728. Then the credits were applied against this, 17 per cent on the first $400, 12 per cent on the remainder up to $100,000, and 9.75 per cent on all over

1. *Treasury Bulletin,* February, 1947, Table 1, Part C, p. A-10, n. 3.

215

$100,000. The credits, which totaled $26,326, were subtracted from $246,-728 to get $220,402. In accordance with the income splitting provision, the latter amount was doubled to get a final tax of $440,804.

In 1950, the effective tax rate curve was raised without touching the regular rate structure. This was done in two ways. First, the tax credit percentages were reduced to 13 per cent, 9 per cent, and 7.3 per cent. In addition, the maximum roof was raised from 77 per cent to 80 per cent of net income. For 1951 and later years, the tax credits were eliminated.

APPENDIX IV

Taxable Income
from Pensions

This appendix is designed to explain the reasoning behind the assumptions used in applying income tax rates to pension income. Tax provisions applying to pensions will be considered in terms of three different periods—1929–1933, 1934–1953, and 1954 to date.

Under the Revenue Act of 1928 which applied to income for the year 1929, the excess of aggregate pension payments over total contributions paid was includable in gross income. In other words, so long as the pension payments were a return of contributions, the income was not taxable, but thereafter the pension became fully taxable.

Starting with the income year 1934, however, the regulations were changed. The new regulations were described by one source as follows:

Instead of exempting all income from annuities until the amounts received exceed the amounts paid as consideration for the contract as under prior law, the Acts of 1934 and 1936 provide that amounts received to the extent of 3% of the aggregate premiums or consideration paid for the annuity are income each year, the remainder being applied against premiums or consideration for the annuity.[1]

The Internal Revenue Code of 1954, which first affected the income year 1954, brought about a further change in taxability of pensions, which spread the amount to be taxed more evenly over the retirement years. The 1954 Code provided that the employee's contributions would be regarded as his investment in the pension contract. The value of the contract was the amount of the pension times the years expected life at retirement. A percentage was obtained by dividing the employee's investment in the contract by its value. This percentage of the pension was excluded every year from taxability.

The hypothetical executive whom we shall use for illustration will be assumed to retire normally at age sixty-five, with a life expectation of fifteen years. We shall assume that on the basis of a known career salary curve the amount of his pension is computed at $22.95 thousand per year, toward which he will have contributed $41.86 thousand. The contributions he has made will amount at 4 per cent to $63.81 thousand, which will buy an annuity at 4 per cent for 15 years at $5.74 thousand. Thus while his actual pension will be $22.95 thousand, the company-paid-for part of it will be $22.95 thousand less $5.74 thousand, or $17.21 thousand.

There are two questions about taxable pension income that may now be raised concerning retirement of our hypothetical executive under differing conditions: (1) would use of the company-paid-for pension instead of the pension subject to tax result in a material difference in taxable income arising from an executive's pension? (2) if pension amounts subject to tax are used, is it important whether all three pension rules are used, or would the simpler regulations under the 1954 Code do equally well for all years?

These questions can be answered from the evidence in the

1. Commerce Clearing House, *U.S. Master Tax Guide 1937*, par. 127, p. 79.

following table, which shows what happens under two major assumptions for three different retirement periods, all the while, for simplicity, considering deductions as zero. Under *Assumption A,* for each retirement period the company-paid-for portion of the pension is treated as being the amount subject to tax each year. Under *Assumption B,* for each retirement period the full amount of the pension is used, the taxable portion being determined by the regulations actually in effect during each of the three retirement periods.

Taxable Income Under 2 Different Assumptions for 3 Different Retirement Periods, Considering Deductions as Zero
(Thousands of Dollars)

RETIREMENT PERIODS

	1 Assumption A	B		2 Assumption A	B		3 Assumption A	B
1929	$ 17.21	$ .00	1945	$ 17.21	$ 1.26	1960	$ 17.21	$ 20.15
1930	17.21	4.04	1946	17.21	2.78	1961	17.21	20.15
1931	17.21	22.95	1947	17.21	22.95	1962	17.21	20.15
1932	17.21	22.95	1948	17.21	22.95	1963	17.21	20.15
1933	17.21	22.95	1949	17.21	22.95	1964	17.21	20.15
1934	17.21	22.95	1950	17.21	22.95	1965	17.21	20.15
1935	17.21	22.95	1951	17.21	22.95	1966	17.21	20.15
1936	17.21	22.95	1952	17.21	22.95	1967	17.21	20.15
1937	17.21	22.95	1953	17.21	22.95	1968	17.21	20.15
1938	17.21	22.95	1954	17.21	22.95	1969	17.21	20.15
1939	17.21	22.95	1955	17.21	22.95	1970	17.21	20.15
1940	17.21	22.95	1956	17.21	22.95	1971	17.21	20.15
1941	17.21	22.95	1957	17.21	22.95	1972	17.21	20.15
1942	17.21	22.95	1958	17.21	22.95	1973	17.21	20.15
1943	17.21	22.95	1959	17.21	22.95	1974	17.21	20.15
	$258.15	$302.39		$258.15	$302.39		$258.15	$302.25

Retirement Period 1 assumes the officer draws retirement pay for the period 1929–1943. *Retirement Period 2* assumes the executive receives a pension during the period 1945–1959. *Retirement Period 3* assumes the receipt of a pension during the years 1960–1974.

Now let us see what happens under the various alternatives. First of all the yearly amounts under *Assumption A* will be $17.21 thousand for every year in all three retirement periods.

219

Under *Assumption B,* the executive starts drawing retirement pay during *Retirement Period 1* under the tax-free return of premiums rule then in effect. He will not be taxed in 1929 since his income consists entirely of a return of contributions. At the end of 1929 there will be left in unreturned contributions $18.91 thousand. The $22.95 thousand pension of 1930 is greater than this by $4.04 thousand. The $4.04 thousand will therefore be fully taxable. For the years 1931–1933, the full $22.95 thousand will be taxable. In 1934 the 3 per cent rule comes into effect, but since all contributions have previously been returned, the pension continues to be fully taxable for the remaining years.

By contrast, if the hypothetical executive starts drawing his pension during *Retirement Period 2,* he will start under the 3 per cent rule. Applying the rule, 3 per cent of the $41.86 thousand contribution is $1.26 thousand, which will be the amount of pension taxable in 1945. The difference between this and the $22.95 thousand pension for 1945, or $21.69 thousand, will be charged against contributions, leaving a balance of contributions amounting to $20.17 thousand. In 1946 another 3 per cent of the original contributions total, or $1.26 thousand, will be taxable, and another $21.69 thousand will be charged against contributions. Since there is, however, a shortage of contributions by $1.52 thousand ($20.17 thousand less $21.69 thousand), the difference is also taxable, bringing 1946 taxable income to $2.78 thousand. And, of course, the years 1947–1953 will be fully taxable. In 1954 this pension falls under the new investment in contract rule. But since the executive must subtract from the amount of investment any amounts received tax-free under the 3 per cent rule, his investment in the contract becomes zero. The result is that his pension for the remaining years continues to be fully taxable.

Finally, if the officer retires in *Retirement Period 3,* which starts in 1960, he comes under the 1954 Code immediately. His investment in the contract will be $41.86 thousand, the total of his contributions toward his pension. The value of the contract will be the pension of $22.95 thousand times fifteen years of expected life at retirement age sixty-five or $344.25 thousand. The investment works out to 12.2 per cent of the value of the contract. The complement of this, or 87.8 per cent times the pension, yields a taxable pension each year of $20.15 thousand.

Thus we may conclude from the table that: (1) the difference in total taxable amounts for the retirement period as between *Assumptions A* and *B* are substantial, being well over $40,000 in each case. It is therefore evident that use of the company-paid-for part of the pension instead of the pension subject to tax would clearly understate the tax effect on the pension; and (2) under *Assumption B* the different tax regulations for the three periods make almost no difference in the total taxable income for the retirment periods, each taken as a whole. Hence, any of the three tax rules could be used for all years. Of the three rules, the simpler regulations provided in the 1954 Code have therefore been employed for the present study.

Bibliography

In our study most of the research was based on information available to the public but not in published form. For example, most of the raw data on executives' compensation came from proxy statements and Annual Reports, Form 10-K, submitted by different companies to the U.S. Securities and Exchange Commission. Other related information came from Current Reports, Form 8-K, or from Form 4, which shows individual stockholdings and transactions. Much information about various company pay plans and about the life histories of individual executives was drawn from the Marvin Scudder Collection of corporate records at Columbia University's Butler Library. These records include many bound volumes mostly containing company annual reports. More recent reports, on microcards, were also used extensively. For certain aspects of executive pay plans, especially in connection with stock options, a useful source was Norman S. Cannon's unpublished 1957 dissertation at Columbia. His dissertation was on "Some Selected Problems in Accounting for Executive Compensation."

223

U.S. Government Publications

Bokelman, W. Robert. *Higher Education Planning and Management Data.* U.S. Department of Health, Education, and Welfare Circular No. 549 (Washington: U.S. Government Printing Office, 1959).

U.S. Congress, House, Committee on Ways and Means. *Individual Income Tax Reduction Act of 1953,* 83rd Cong., 1st Sess., 1953, H. Report 49 to accompany H.R. 1.

U.S. Federal Trade Commission. *Report on Compensation of Officers and Directors of Certain Corporations.* Pursuant to S. Res. 75, 73rd Cong., 1st Sess., presented to the Senate February 26, 1934.

U.S. Internal Revenue Service. Release on expense accounts, December 29, 1959.

————. *Statistics of Income, Corporate Income Tax Returns* (Washington: U.S. Government Printing Office, 1928–1954).

————. *Statistics of Income, Individual Income Tax Returns* (Washington: U.S. Government Printing Office, 1929–1957).

U.S. Securities and Exchange Commission, *Annual Report* (Washington: U.S. Government Printing Office, 1935–1956).

————. *General Rules and Regulations under the Securities Act of 1933,* 1935–1958.

————. *General Rules and Regulations under the Securities Exchange Act of 1934,* 1935–1958.

————. Instructions for preparing Annual Report, Form 10-K, 1935–1958.

————. *Official Summary of Transactions and Holdings,* 1935–1958.

————. *Securities Traded on Exchanges under the Securities Exchange Act,* 1935–1958.

————. Division of Corporate Regulation. *Proposed Findings and Conclusions of the Division of Corporate Regulation in the Matter of Middle South Utilities, Inc.,* File No. 70–3777.

U.S. Treasury Department. "Lists of Individuals Receiving from Corporations for Personal Services in Excess of $75,000." 1941–1945.

————. *Treasury Bulletin,* February 1947, Table 1, Part G, pp. A-7 through A-15.

Annual Periodicals

Annual Dividend Record (New York: Standard and Poor's Corporation, 1958).

224

Facts and Figures on Government Finance (New York: Tax Foundation, 1944–1959).

Federal Taxes, 1958 (New York and other: Commerce Clearing House, 1958).

Life Insurance Fact Book (New York: Institute of Life Insurance, 1959).

Moody's Industrial Manual (New York: Moody's Investors Service, 1919–1958).

New York Times Index, bound volumes, and microfilms, 1928–1958.

Poor's Register of Directors and Executives (New York: Standard and Poor's Corporation, 1935–1960).

Prentice-Hall Federal Tax Course (New York: Prentice-Hall, 1937–1958).

Security Price Index Record (New York: Standard and Poor's Corporation, 1957 and 1959 supplement).

Standard Corporation Descriptions (New York: Standard and Poor's Corporation, 1942–1958).

A Study of Industrial Retirement Plans (New York: Banker's Trust Company, 1943–1959).

U.S. Master Tax Guide (Chicago: Commerce Clearing House, 1937–1958).

Who's Who in America. 31 vols (Chicago: A. N. Marquis, 1899—XV to XXX, 1928–1959).

Who Was Who. 3 vols (Chicago: A. N. Marquis, 1897—I and II, 1897–1950).

Books

Baker, John C. *Executive Salaries and Bonus Plans* (New York and London: McGraw-Hill, 1938).

Bogen, Jules I. (ed.). *Financial Handbook.* 3rd ed. (New York: The Ronald Press, 1957).

Burgess, Leonard R., and Neuhoff, Malcolm C. *Managing Company Airplanes.* Studies in Business Policy No. 65 (New York: National Industrial Conference Board, 1954).

Butters, J. Keith, Thompson, Laurence E., and Bollinger, Lynn L. *Effects of Taxation—Investments by Individuals* (Boston: Graduate School of Business Administration, Harvard University, 1953).

Compensation of Top Executives. Studies in Labor Statistics No. 17 (New York: National Industrial Conference Board, 1956).

Executive Compensation. Studies in Labor Statistics No. 12 (New York: National Industrial Conference Board, 1954).

Greenewalt, Crawford H. *The Uncommon Man* (New York, Toronto, and London: McGraw-Hill, 1959).

Hall, Challis A., Jr. *Effects of Taxation—Executive Compensation and Retirement Plans* (Boston: Graduate School of Business Administration, Harvard University, 1951).

Kaplan, A. D. H. *Big Enterprise in a Competitive System* (Washington: The Brookings Institution, 1954).

Knowlton, P. A. *Profit Sharing Patterns* (Evanston, Illinois: Profit Sharing Research Foundation, 1954).

Latimer, Murray Webb. *Industrial Pension Systems in the United States and Canada.* 2 vols (New York: Industrial Relations Counselors, 1932).

Livingston, J. A. *The American Stockholder* (Philadelphia and New York: J. B. Lippincott, 1938).

Martucci, Nicholas L. A., and Fox, Harland. *Compensation of Top Executives.* Studies in Personnel Policy No. 173 (New York: National Industrial Conference Board, 1959).

Moore, Justin H. *Handbook of Financial Mathematics* (New York: Prentice-Hall, 1929).

Neuhoff, Malcolm C. *Executive Expense Accounts.* Studies in Business Policy No. 67 (New York: National Industrial Conference Board, 1954).

Roberts, David R. *Executive Compensation* (Glencoe: The Free Press of Glencoe, 1959).

Sanders, Thomas H. *Effects of Taxation on Executives* (Boston: Graduate School of Business Administration, Harvard University, 1951).

Seidman, Jacob S. *Seidman's Legislative History of the Federal Income Tax Laws, 1938–1861* (New York: Prentice-Hall, 1938).

226

Name Index

AFL-CIO, Industrial Union Dept., 76
Allied Chemical, 211
Aluminum Company of America, 2, 33, 44, 87, 97, 135–136, 139, 159, 211
American Smelting and Refining, 101, 102, 181, 211
American Tobacco, 44, 127, 211
Anaconda Company, 12, 54, 97, 127, 130, 135–136, 159, 211
Armour and Company, 5, 211

Baker, John C., 23, 45, 125, 190–191
Beaton, Kendall, 62
Bethlehem Steel, 2, 43–45, 125, 127–128, 130, 134–137, 143, 159, 182, 200, 211
Bokelman, W. Robert, 206
Bollinger, Lynn L., 197
Brewster, Kingman, 192
Burgess, Leonard R., 111
Burns, Arthur F., vii, 195
Bursk, E. C., 163
Butters, J. Keith, 197, 203

Cannon, Norman S., 197, 223
Chrysler, 31, 44, 87, 99, 100, 127–128, 134–137, 139, 158–160, 181, 211
Cities Service, 127, 135–136, 159, 211

Dockeray, James C., 103
Dodd, David L., 90
Dow Chemical, 54, 127, 211
Doyle, William A., 88–89
Du Pont, 32, 37, 44, 47, 90–91, 99, 125–131, 133, 135–136, 138, 153, 159–160, 164–165, 200, 205, 211

Eiteman, Wilford J., 36–37

Ford, 44, 87, 128, 134–137, 159–160, 211
Fox, Harland, 2, 97

General Electric, 35, 44, 87, 97, 126–129, 132, 134–137, 150–151, 159, 194, 202, 204, 211

General Motors, 2, 32, 37, 44, 46–47, 90–91, 99, 126–129, 134–138, 150, 158–160, 192, 200, 204, 211
Ginzberg, Eli, vii
Goodyear Tire and Rubber, 44, 87, 127, 135–136, 139, 159, 211
Graham, Benjamin, 90
Greenewalt, Crawford H., 164, 165, 190
Griswold, Erwin N., 161, 198, 204
Gulf Oil, 29–30, 32, 44, 87, 126–128, 130, 132, 134–138, 159, 211

Hall, Challis A., Jr., 130, 190, 192, 195
Hayes, Albert J., 102
Hobbs, G. Warfield, III, vii
Husband, William H., 103
Hyde, George G., 165

International Business Machines, 5, 44, 134–137, 159, 195, 211
International Harvester, 44, 58–59, 127–128, 130–131, 134–136, 159, 211
International Paper, 5, 97–98, 102, 125, 211

Jones and Laughlin Steel, 211

Kaplan, A. D. H., 5, 209, 210
Kaysen, Carl, 194
Kennecott Copper, 211

Lasser, J. K., 47, 184, 191–192, 195
Latimer, Murray Webb, 226
Livingston, Joseph A., 182, 193, 206

Martucci, Nicholas L. A., 2, 46, 107, 109, 110, 192
Mills, Frederick C., 114
Murray, Roger F., vii

Neuhoff, Malcolm G., 103, 106–107, 111

Patton, Arch, 5
Phillips Petroleum, 87, 97–98, 127, 135–136, 159, 212
Pullman Company, 212

R. J. Reynolds Tobacco, 46, 212
Republic Steel, 54, 78, 87, 135–136, 159, 167, 212
Richmond, Samuel B., vii
Roberts, David R., 1, 71, 180–183, 193, 195
Rothschild, V. Henry, 47, 184, 191–192, 195
Ruml, Beardsley, 104

Sanders, Thomas H., 107–108, 180–184, 186, 188
Sayles, Leonard R., vii
Scott, Ira O., vii
Seidman, Jacob S., 226
Shell Oil, 61–62, 125–127, 135–136, 138–139, 159, 212
Shoup, Carl S., vii, 205
Sinclair Oil, 87, 130–133, 135–136, 159, 212
Smith, Dan T., 149, 202, 203
Smith, Frank P., 36–37
Smyth, Richard C., 43, 47, 192
Socony Mobil Oil, 97, 127, 135–136, 159, 200, 212
Standard Oil (Ind.), 87, 97–98, 125, 127, 135–136, 159, 200, 212
Standard Oil of California, 127, 132, 135–136, 138–139, 159, 200, 212
Standard Oil of New Jersey, 87, 89, 125–127, 132, 134–136, 138, 159, 200, 212
Swift and Company, 5, 212

Texas Company, 33–35, 44, 97, 127, 131–133, 135–136, 139, 159, 212
Thompson, Laurence E., 197
Tidewater Oil, 97, 212

Union Carbide, 79–82, 86–87, 93, 126–127, 135–136, 138, 159, 200, 212
U.S. Rubber, 212
U.S. Steel, 53, 87, 126–127, 129, 131–133, 135–137, 159, 182, 200, 212

Westinghouse Electric, 35, 44, 127, 134–136, 138, 159, 212

Youngstown Sheet and Tube, 44, 212

Subject Index

Bonuses
  and conspicuous service, 47–48
  currently paid bonuses, 26
  deferred, income values of, 26–35
    (*see also* Income values)
  and profits, 46–47, 192
  and salaries, 40, 43–44, 192
  and stockholders, 44–47, 192
  trends in (1929–1958), 36–42

Career salary curve, 13–24
  and age when joined company, 14–15
  and assumption as to starting pay, 16
  curves for one company, 16–18
  and income values of deferred benefits, 9–10, 24
  lower tail of, 18–21
  theoretical alternatives, 18–20
  upper tail of, 21–24
  and year when joined company, 15–16

Differentials
  alternative methods, 166–169
  average pay, before taxes, 168, 170
  dollar, 170, 172–174, 188–189
  future outlook, 177–178, 190
  percentage, 174–177, 189–190
  standards, 164–168

Executives
  age retired, 68, 71, 180
  age when joined company, 14, 180
  career salary curve, 13–24
  and earlier retirement, 68–71, 186, 194–195
  expense accounts, 102–112
  length of service, 180, 186–188
  market for, 180–182
  mobility, 179–182, 186–188, 190, 192–195
  pay and performance, 179–197
  pay trends, compared to those in professional occupations, 116
  role as investor *vs.* role as executive, 32, 35, 73, 75–76, 84

229

minimization of, 141–154
and policies, 200–205
tax calculations, 213–216
Total pay package, 114–116, 183, 185
differentials in, 168–178, 188–190, 197
five selected companies, by pay item, 130–133
items not included in pay package, 95–112
performance of individual companies, 122–129, 183

regrouped into pay package elements, 117–119
and taxes, 154–160, 202, 204
before and after taxes, in individual companies (1958), 133–140
before and after taxes, by major pay element, 119–124, 191, 193–194
before taxes, by major pay element, in individual companies (1958), 136–140